SOLUTIONS:

A Guide to Better Problem Solving

SOLUTIONS:
A Guide to Better Problem Solving

Steven R. Phillips, Ph.D.
William H. Bergquist, Ph.D.

Pfeiffer
& COMPANY

San Diego • Toronto • Amsterdam • Sydney

Copyright © 1987 by University Associates, Inc.
ISBN: 0-88390-205-2
Library of Congress Catalog Card Number: 87-5894
Printed in the United States of America

Library of Congress Cataloging-in-Publication Data
Phillips, Steven R.
     Solutions: a guide to better problem solving.

     1. Problem solving. I. Bergquist, William H.
II. Title.
HD30.29.P48   1987   658.4′03   87-5894
ISBN 0-88390-205-2

Senior Editor: Carol Nolde

Cover Designer
   & Production Artist: Ann Beaulieu

Book Design & Layout: Carol Nolde and Ann Beaulieu

To Doug Pearson

Preface: A Fable for Our Times

A peasant complains to his priest that his little hut is horribly overcrowded. The priest advises him to move his cow into the house, the next week to take in his sheep, and the next week his horse. The peasant now complains even more bitterly about his lot. Then the priest advises him to let out the cow, the next week the sheep, and the next week the horse. At the end the peasant gratefully thanks the priest for lightening his burdensome life.[1]

This old folk tale is based on an ancient phenomenon: In attempting to solve problems, people often ask others for help. At times they feel better about their problems after receiving such help, not because the problems have been solved but because they have gained new perspectives on those problems. The two of us, as authors of this book, propose that we can be of help to you as you confront and solve problems in your daily life. We believe that we can provide you with something more than a new perspective on the problems you face.

In this book you will be introduced to *integrated problem management*, a set of techniques and strategies that we believe constitutes one of the most powerful and comprehensive approaches to problem solving available today. Unlike the peasant, you will learn to make choices that will yield desirable and anticipated consequences.

Although people have been thinking about problem analysis and problem solving for many years, integrated problem management brings together, for the first time, a variety of different approaches to the solution of personal and professional problems. This integration nevertheless rests on the previous work of several individuals whom we would like to acknowledge. The work of Charles Kepner and Benjamin Tregoe (1981) in *The New Rational Manager*[2] has been important in formulating the process of what we call in Chapter 8 "causal/resource analysis" and in identifying potential problems as discussed in Chapter 11. In addition, the work of Gordon Prince at Synectics in Cambridge, Massachusetts, has helped us in understanding the process of creative problem solving discussed in Chapter 9.

---

[1] From *Work and Its Discontents* by D. Bell, 1956, Boston: Beacon Press.

[2] *The New Rational Manager* by C.H. Kepner and B.B. Tregoe, 1981, Princeton, NJ: Kepner-Tregoe.

The basic problem-solving model on which this book is based was first created by Dr. Fred Fosmire and Dr. John Wallen. Between 1966 and 1971 these two men established a remarkable collaboration that brought together the earlier thinking of several other people. Fosmire had been strongly influenced by the work of Charles Morris (1964) as presented in *Signification and Significance: A Study of the Relations of Signs and Values*[3] and by the thinking of Forrest L. Brissey, his colleague at the University of Oregon. Wallen drew on the work of Mary Parker Follett on conflict resolution and the "interaction process analysis" of Robert F. Bales. It was during a series of workshops conducted by the National Training Laboratories in the late Sixties and early Seventies that Fosmire and Wallen created the "situation, target, proposal" approach to problem solving. Their work has made this book possible, and we wish to acknowledge and express our appreciation for the invaluable contribution these two men have made to integrated problem management.

Finally, this work would not have been possible without the support of Doug Pearson, manager of employee development at Panhandle Eastern Corporation in Houston, Texas. It was Doug's dissatisfaction with the limitations of rational problem solving that brought us together with him and his colleague, Rebecca McDonald, at Panhandle to develop an alternate approach, an approach that ultimately became integrated problem management. We are grateful for their contributions to and support of this work.

The process of problem solving is very much like a journey, not one through a physical landscape but rather through an interior world of values and desires, of perceptions about the way things are and the way people would like them to be. We welcome you on that journey and look forward to sharing some of the exciting ideas that you will discover with us along the way.

Steven R. Phillips
Corvallis, Oregon

William H. Bergquist
San Francisco, California

December, 1986

---

[3]*Signification and Significance: A Study of the Relations of Signs and Values* by C. Morris, 1964, Cambridge, MA: MIT Press.

Twenty Useful Questions in Integrated Problem Management

Phase 1: Identifying the Target

   1. What am I trying to accomplish?

   2. If the problem were solved, what exactly would be happening?

Phase 2: Assessing the Situation

   3. Who is involved in the problem?

   4. What exactly is wrong?

   5. Where is the problem taking place?

   6. When did the problem begin?

   7. When was the problem first observed?

   8. What is the extent and/or the pattern of the problem?

Phase 3: Conducting Causal/Resource Analysis

   9. What is different?

  10. What is the same?

  11. What resources exist to solve the problem?

  12. What is the most likely cause of the problem?

Phase 4: Generating Proposals

  13. What are some ways to move from the present situation to the target?

Phase 5: Selecting Proposals

  14. Is the proposal appropriate?

  15. Is the proposal attainable?

  16. Is the proposal attractive?

  17. Is the proposal adaptable?

Phase 6: Planning and Implementing

  18. What might go wrong?

  19. What can be done now to prevent that from happening?

  20. What should be done if that does happen?

Contents

1

What This Book Is About

In our work with a wide variety of individuals, groups, and organizations over the last fifteen years, we have come to one inescapable conclusion: Most people are not very good problem solvers. They either muddle through, do nothing, adapt, or produce "solutions" that often make things worse. Something is seriously wrong with the way in which people try to solve problems.

From interviews and discussions with hundreds of managers, employees, and average citizens over those same fifteen years, we have learned something else: Most people are willing to settle for things just as they are.

Of course problem solving is hard. As M. Scott Peck (1978) writes in *The Road Less Travelled*:

> ...the process of confronting and solving problems is a painful one. Problems, depending upon their nature, evoke in us frustration or grief or sadness or loneliness or guilt or regret or anger or fear or anxiety or anguish or despair. These are uncomfortable feelings, often very uncomfortable, often as painful as any kind of physical pain. (p. 16)

Effective problem solving requires the courage to confront these feelings, the commitment to do something, and above all the willingness to assume responsibility for solving the problem.

How much easier it is to complain about the way things are than to have the courage to change them. Most people prefer an unsatisfactory present to an uncertain future. As Shakespeare's Hamlet put it almost four hundred years ago, we would rather bear those ills we have than fly to those we know not of.

But what if an individual, a group, or an entire organization honestly wants to change? We have learned at least one more thing over the years: Even if people's intentions are the best, most do not possess an adequate set of problem-solving skills. With all the good intentions in the world, people often discover that where they end up is not where they wanted to be at all. Consider the following examples:

1. ***The case of the government forms.*** Several dozen clerical workers in a large government agency were required to produce the same report once a month. The problem was that these workers, spread over several floors of a large office building, each processed these forms differently. The group whose responsibility it was to collate the information from all the forms was faced with an increasingly impossible task.

To solve this problem, those in charge held a one-day workshop to review the proper procedures and to involve all of the workers in a series of case studies that required them to complete the form in the same way each time. Although the situation did improve the next month, it was not long before the workers went back to their old ways of doing things. When the expenses of conducting the workshop and of taking workers off the job were calculated, the workshop ultimately cost the agency approximately $30,000; and afterward the problem was as bad as ever.

About seven months after the workshop, one of the clerical workers wrote a note to her supervisor pointing out that the data entered on this particular form came from three different sources—one federal, one state, and one local—and suggested that the form would be easier to complete if it were revised to indicate which of the three sources should supply which data. When the form was changed to present the information from the three sources in three separate sections, the problem disappeared.

2. *The case of the private university.* In completing a required ten-year plan for the state board of education, a small private university in New York had spent literally thousands of faculty and administrative hours debating the issue of whether or not the university should grow from its enrollment of 2,500 students to a maximum of 3,000 students by the end of the decade. According to various parties, several issues were at stake: the historical character and mission of the institution, the importance of the position of the university in the local community, the relationship of the university to a local two-year community college, and the ecology of the valley in which the university was located.

Two years after the completion of the ten-year plan, the university was facing drastic budget cuts and the prospect of faculty and administrative layoffs as enrollment slipped for the second straight year to below 2,000 students.

3. *The case of the regional sales manager.* Within six weeks of the appointment of a new regional sales manager, sales in that region began to drop. When sales continued to fall over the next two months, the new manager was released and replaced with a more experienced manager from the home office.

Sales continued to drop for another month but then improved when the major employer in the region began rehiring its employees to meet a new government contract. Those employees had been released at the completion of the previous contract, the same time that the first manager took over and sales began to decline.

4. *The case of the vacationing couple.* A news story was published concerning a bicycle trip taken by a young couple from Minneapolis, Minnesota, to Bremerton, Washington. The husband and wife had made the long trip because they wanted to visit the *U.S.S. Missouri* at the Bremerton Naval Shipyard. When they arrived in Bremerton, they discovered that several months earlier the battleship had been moved to Long Beach, California, for refitting and recommissioning.

5. *The case of the paint manufacturer.* A large midwestern paint manufacturer installed two new, sophisticated blending machines in September, 1982. Both worked up to specification for about six weeks, at which time Number Two began to malfunction. The trouble lasted all winter, then disappeared. Number One continued to operate perfectly. When the problem with Number Two began again the next November, the manufacturer spent over $5,000 overhauling the machine. Problems continued, however, until the spring and then once again disappeared.

When the same problems began again the next fall, one of the operators suggested that it might have something to do with the weather. Number One was positioned against a heated, inside wall, while Number Two sat against an outside wall. When this possibility was investigated, it was discovered that a key chemical ran against that outside wall and that its significantly lower temperature during the winter was the cause of the problem. The cost of correcting the situation was just over $700.

In each of these cases, in dozens of others we have seen, and in the scores of others that you have undoubtedly experienced, well-intentioned people either analyzed the problem incorrectly, made the wrong decision, or were unable to avoid future problems. As we said at the beginning of this chapter, most people are not very good problem solvers.

But, of course, this situation can be changed. In this book we present a process called *integrated problem management,* a set of problem-solving tools and strategies that, when used together, constitute the most comprehensive approach to problem solving available today. If this process had been used in each of the cases just presented, each problem could have been solved or avoided with far less human and financial cost. Because integrated problem management constitutes a significant departure from other problem-solving strategies presently available, we would like to identify at the outset the four basic assumptions that lie behind our approach.

ASSUMPTION 1: PROBLEM SOLVING SHOULD BE HOLISTIC

As Marilyn Ferguson (1980) has demonstrated in *The Aquarian Conspiracy,* the frontiers of research in such diverse areas as medicine, education, politics, communication, and values all suggest that people are moving toward a much more integrated view of what it means to be human. Fragmentation, disintegration, and the inevitable either/or choices that the past has forced on people are giving way to a new sense of the whole.

Until now fragmentation has been evident in the two intellectual traditions that have dominated our thinking about problem solving. One of these traditions is rational, logical, and linear. This tradition is characterized by what has come to be known as "left-brain" thinking. For most people there seems to be some association between the left side of the cerebral cortex and the "reasonable" self. It appears that the left brain remembers names, likes structure, relies on language, rarely uses metaphors or analogies, and solves problems by breaking them down into their component parts. Left-brain problem solving most often begins with a clear specification of the problem and a description of how that problem deviates from an acceptable standard. A comparison of the problem with that standard then leads to an identification of the single most likely cause of the problem. The result is a neat, logical sequence of steps for solving a neat, logical problem.

The second intellectual tradition is more creative, intuitive, and imaginative. This tradition is associated with the right brain rather than the left. The right brain remembers faces rather than names, is more spontaneous than the left, relies on images rather than language, frequently thinks in metaphors and analogies, and solves problems by looking at relationships rather than parts. Right-brain problem solving can begin almost anywhere and move in almost any direction, often in a playful or even humorous manner. Perhaps the most well-known right-brain strategy for problem solving is "brainstorming," through which a small group of people can produce a wide variety of possible solutions, some of which will be impractical and even foolish and others of which may constitute genuine creative breakthroughs.

Until now people have been taught to be either *rational* problem solvers or *creative* problem solvers. A holistic approach, however, would suggest that problem solving needs to be balanced between the left and the right brains. Rational problem solving works for a certain range of problems in which a clear deviation from standard can be identified. But in situations in which the problem involves the development of a prototype or product that has never existed before, or when the cause of the problem is clear but its solution is obscure, or when no one is certain about what is actually wanted, rational problem solving is of limited help. What is needed in these situations is the creativity and vision of the right brain.

Most problems, of course, require the use of both sides of the brain. People must be rational at times and creative at times; but throughout the problem-solving process they must be clear about what they want. Integrated problem management brings together for the first time the best of what is known about rational *and* creative problem solving into a single comprehensive model. This process can be used to address any problem an individual, a group, or an organization will ever encounter.

ASSUMPTION 2:
MOST PROBLEMS ARE COMPLEX

In *Beyond the Quick Fix*, Kilmann (1985) describes two contrasting world views. The first, a view of the world as a simple machine, "argues for single efforts at change, much like replacing one defective part in some mechanical apparatus: The one defective part can be replaced without affecting any other part" (p. 8). As Kilmann points out, this approach "works only for fixing a physical, nonliving system" (p. 8) and is simply inadequate for dealing with "a living, breathing organization" (p. 8). In contrast is a quite different view, one of the world as a "complex hologram" that includes often-hidden cultures, beliefs, and assumptions, such as those that exist in today's organizations.

We believe that the world views people hold have a profound effect on the way in which they approach problems. If people see the world in simple, mechanical terms, they see problems as relatively simple puzzles that can be solved with some sense of finality; and they seek those problem-solving strategies that hold out the promise of providing clear and defined solutions. If, on the other hand, people see the world in terms of complexity, they see problems as correspondingly complex, interrelated, and perhaps incapable of simple solution; such people seek ways of managing problems rather than solving them.

Rational approaches to problem solving hold out the promise of simple, definable solutions to relatively simple, definable problems. Since, as Kilmann suggests, "American engineers are taught the value of analysis, of pulling apart, but not of synthesis, of putting together" (p. 9), and since most "American students are taught to appreciate mathematics" (p. 9) rather than metaphors, this approach holds great attraction for the would-be rational manager. But the problems that managers encounter in the real world are not as simple as those presented in case studies; consequently, either the complexity of real problems is distorted or ignored so that these problems can be "solved," or managers put aside what they have learned in case studies as irrelevant and muddle through as before. One of the basic intentions of integrated problem management is to provide a way of approaching problems that acknowledges their complexity and that does not offer the illusion of the quick fix.

ASSUMPTION 3:
PROBLEM SOLVING IS SITUATIONAL

In our workshops on integrated problem management, we teach problem solving as a six-phase process potentially involving numerous separate steps. When we first present this model, the common reaction is astonishment at the number of steps involved; but we quickly point out that no problem requires the use of all of the steps. Depending on the situation, most problems can be solved by using one or two steps or, at the most, one or two phases. As one becomes skilled in the use of this process, one selects the one or two elements needed, does what is necessary to manage the problem, and then gets back to work. Unlike most other approaches to problem solving, integrated problem management does not require adherence to a rigid set of steps but rather provides a *range* of strategies and tools to be selected and deployed as the situation demands.

ASSUMPTION 4:
THERE IS NO SUBSTITUTE
FOR EFFECTIVE INTERPERSONAL SKILLS

We firmly believe that if serious conflict exists in a relationship, a group, or an organization and if the individuals involved in the conflict are unable or unwilling to communicate openly with and listen to one another, then no problem-solving strategy will be of much help. Effective problem solving requires both an effective *method* for solving problems and an effective *process* of interpersonal communication. Building a successful relationship, team, or organization requires attention to both dimensions.

This book can teach you how to become a better problem solver. It requires you to study, work, and practice the process presented. Successful problem solving can be rewarding, but it can also be very hard work. Before undertaking such a task, think for a moment about your investment in your problem. What are the advantages of not changing, of not being responsible? They may well outweigh the effort you will need to make to change things. If you do choose to change, however, we wish you success and we believe this book will help.

REFERENCES

Ferguson, M. (1980). *The Aquarian conspiracy.* Los Angeles: J.P. Tarcher.

Kilmann, R.H. (1985). *Beyond the quick fix.* San Francisco: Jossey-Bass.

Peck, M.S. (1978). *The road less travelled.* New York: Simon and Schuster.

The Problem with Problem Solving

The following example illustrates the way in which most people go about solving problems:

□ Larry Stevens is the manager of the furniture department in a large department store. For some time now he has been having problems with Frank Foster, his assistant manager in the department. The issue has finally come to a head, and Larry has just this morning written a detailed memo to Nancy Miller, the new store manager, concerning the situation.

Larry has a meeting tomorrow morning with Nancy to decide what to do about Frank. Larry expects Nancy to ask him for some kind of recommendation; but he is uncertain about what, if anything, he should suggest.

On his way out of the store this afternoon, Larry has stopped into the office of his friend, Bill Johnson, another department manager, for advice. Bill invites him into his office.

Bill: Hi, Larry. Come on in. How are you doing?

Larry: Actually, not too great. I've got a meeting with Nancy tomorrow, and I'm not sure what I'm going to do.

Bill: Yeah, I know. She's sometimes difficult to work with. I sure liked the old manager better.

Larry: Yes, but that's not the problem. The problem is Frank Foster, my assistant. I may have let things slide there a little too long, but he's just not working out.

Bill: So what's the problem? Why don't you just let him go?

Larry: I probably should, but somehow I don't think that would be fair.

Bill: Why not? You've given him enough of a chance to prove himself, haven't you?

Larry: Well, I'm not sure. I did move him along pretty fast. I even skipped sending him to the two-week training course that headquarters offers for new managers.

Bill: No kidding? I thought that was almost a requirement. Sounds to me like that's your problem.

Larry: Could be. I'm just not sure.

Bill: Look, we both know how good the course is. And from what I hear lately, it's even better than it was when we took it.

Larry: I know it's a good course, but . . . .

Bill: Take my advice—send him off to the course. Then if he doesn't shape up, well, at least you've given him a chance.

Larry: That certainly sounds reasonable.

Bill: And my guess would be that Nancy will like that solution. You know how hot she is on training.

Larry: That's for sure. Well, thanks. I guess that's what I should try.

Bill: I'd bet on it. See you tomorrow. And good luck with your meeting.

Larry: Thanks for your help.

Larry leaves Bill's office for home. The expression on his face is not optimistic.

This example is typical of what happens every day. Usually when confronted with a problem, a person does one of two things: He or she either ignores it in the hope that it will go away or immediately attempts to come up with a solution. Both of these things seem to be happening in the example. Larry, by his own admission, has "let things slide a little too long." Like many people, he has at first ignored the problem. But this time it has not gone away. Larry's back is now against the wall; he must do something.

Bill is more than happy to "help." His first suggestion is to fire Frank. When that piece of advice is rejected (as most advice usually is), he then grabs at the first available cause of the problem, Frank's lack of training. This "solution" is almost forced on Larry, who seems no more satisfied with this than with the first.

It may turn out that firing Frank or sending him to the training course for new managers is the best solution to Larry's problem. But it may also turn out that neither of these "solutions" is adequate or acceptable. If Larry were to fire Frank, does he have a suitable replacement? If Frank were to go to the training course as suggested, can the department afford to be without him for two weeks? Besides, when is the next course being offered?

Bill's approach of grasping the first likely solution, although typical of what many people do every day, is probably not going to work. He has not taken the time to find out what Larry wants in the way of a solution, nor has he found out very much about what is actually wrong. Trial-and-error problem solving may from time to time bear spectacular successes, but more often than not it will result in failure. There must be a better way.

There Is a Better Way

In this chapter Bill and Larry try again. But this time they employ some of the powerful ideas presented in this book and are more successful in solving the problem. You, too, are going to be involved in solving Larry's problem. In the following pages you will be presented with five activities; complete each of them in order before you proceed to the next. For each activity, read through the material and complete the assignment in the space provided by writing what your response to Larry's problem would be.

Note that here and quite frequently throughout this book you are asked to complete various tasks. We regard this involvement on your part as one of the most important aspects of this book. We do not think that you can learn to be a better problem solver by just reading about problem solving; instead you need to participate actively by working on real problems. We encourage you, therefore, to take the time to use this book, to write in it, and to be involved. If you do, you will receive far more for your efforts than if you do not.

ACTIVITY 1

☐ Larry Stevens is the manager of the furniture department in a large department store. For some time now he has been having problems with Frank Foster, his assistant manager in the department. The issue has finally come to a head; and Larry has just this morning written a detailed memo to Nancy Miller, the new store manager, concerning the situation.

Larry has a meeting tomorrow morning with Nancy to decide what to do about Frank. Larry expects Nancy to ask him for some kind of recommendation; but he is uncertain about what, if anything, he should suggest.

On his way out of the store this afternoon, Larry has stopped into the office of his friend, Bill Johnson, another department manager, for advice. Bill invites him into his office.

Bill: Hi, Larry. Come on in. How are you doing?

Larry: Actually, not too great. I've got a meeting with Nancy tomorrow, and I'm not sure what I'm going to do.

Bill: What's the problem?

Larry: It's Frank Foster, my assistant department manager. He just doesn't seem to be working out.

Bill: And just how is Nancy involved?

Larry: She's heard of the problem, of course. And she and I talked a bit about it yesterday. That's when she asked me to put my perception of what was wrong in writing so that we could meet tomorrow to decide what to do.

Bill: And?

Larry: Well, I wrote a memo. I've got a copy right here in my briefcase. I was going to read it over again tonight at home—maybe get some new ideas.

Bill: Do you mind if I read it?

Larry: Sure, here it is. Take your time. I'm going to get a cup of coffee.

The memorandum reads as follows:

MEMO TO: Nancy Miller, Store Manager
FROM: Larry Stevens, Manager, Furniture Dept.
SUBJECT: Frank Foster
DATE: October 21

The purpose of this memo is to put into writing a summary of our October 20th conversation concerning Frank Foster. As we agreed yesterday, Frank has been a valuable employee; and our intention is to review his case most carefully before taking any further action, disciplinary or otherwise.

Last November Frank began working for us as a part-time salesperson in the Furniture Department, assisting with the Christmas rush. I was so impressed with his eagerness and ability to work under pressure that I offered him a full-time position, which he accepted in mid-January. He worked out well in that position, and in May I promoted him to assistant department manager. Even though he seemed to be doing equally well at the new job at first, we are both aware of the amount of sick time he has taken since late August and of the increasing number of customer complaints we have had concerning Frank this fall. I have talked with him a couple of times within the last month, and he assures me that he needs only a little more time to adjust to his new position. I realize that he is under some pressure. Although we have had no complaints for the last week, you and I have agreed that something needs to be done.

I am certain that part of the difficulty stems from Frank's rapid move from salesperson to assistant department manager. The average time in the position of salesperson before promotion is about eighteen months to two years. But with the resignation of my previous assistant manager, I needed someone right away and thought that Frank could handle the job. Also, I knew his wife was expecting their first child in June and was sure they could use the additional money. Because of the pressure then and the subsequent introduction of the new fall line in August, I have not been able to find time to send Frank to the two-week course that Corporate offers for new managers. This lack of training may have contributed to the problem. Also, as you know, I have been spending a considerable amount of time orienting you to the operation of our company since your arrival this past June; as a result, I may not have spent enough time with Frank. Finally, if we were to fire Frank at this time (which I am not necessarily suggesting), I have no one with whom to replace him.

I hope these comments accurately reflect our conversation and the situation. I am, of course, willing to take whatever action you feel is appropriate.

Bill: Well, that memo certainly covers the situation.

Larry: Thanks. Now if I can just figure out what to suggest to Nancy tomorrow. . . .

Bill: So your first problem is to decide what you're going to do at the meeting with Nancy.

Larry: Right.

Bill: What are some of the things you've thought of suggesting?

If you were in Larry's position, what are some of the things you might think of suggesting to Nancy? Write your suggestions in the space that follows.

ACTIVITY 2

☐ Larry has just described several options, and Bill has listed them:

- Doing nothing in the hope that the situation will improve on its own;
- Firing Frank and finding a replacement;
- Moving Frank back to sales and finding a new assistant;
- Finding out more about the nature of the complaints against Frank;
- Sending Frank to the training course;
- Finding out if Frank is experiencing problems at home; and
- Trying to spend less time with Nancy so that he can train Frank himself.

Bill looks over the completed list and tells Larry his reaction:

Bill: You have quite a few alternatives here.

Larry: I know. But I'm not really satisfied with any of them . . . or confident that any one of them will work.

Bill: I can see what you mean. Maybe you could describe for me what you'd like to accomplish. If this problem were solved to your satisfaction, what would be going on?

Problem solving can often be improved if one takes the time to outline objectives. From your point of view, what would be happening at this department store if the problem were to be solved? Write your answer in the space that follows.

ACTIVITY 3

☐ The conversation continues with Larry's response to Bill's question about what would be happening if the problem were solved:

Larry: That's easy. Frank would be doing his job well. There just wouldn't be any more problems.

Bill: How would you know if Frank were doing his job well?

Larry: Well, I guess. . .oh, I know. We wouldn't have any more customer complaints about him.

Bill: And what about his sick time?

Larry: That's right. We'd get his sick time back down to where it should be.

Bill: Where is that?

Larry: No more than the store average? How would that be?

Bill (smiling): He's your assistant, Larry. But that sounds reasonable to me. So a better way of saying that you want Frank to be doing his job well would be to say that you want to eliminate customer complaints about him and to get his sick time down to or below the store average. Anything else?

Larry: No, I think that would about cover it. It's not as simple as it looks, is it?

Bill: Well, no. How about Nancy? Is she part of your picture of how you'd like things to be?

Larry: What do you mean?

Bill: You said you were spending a lot of time with her.

Larry: That's right. I guess if I could have everything I want, she would be settled in and I would be spending most of my time back in my department.

Bill: You said "if I could have everything I want." Is there some kind of conflict here that makes you think you can't have everything you want?

Larry: I think so. I can't get both Nancy and Frank settled into their jobs without spending time with them. And I don't have enough time to spend what I'd like with each of them.

Bill: Let's not worry about what you're going to do just yet. You're saying that getting Frank's job performance where you want it is the higher priority for now.

Larry: That's right.

Bill: But you could fire Frank or send him back to sales. Those are a couple of the options you mentioned.

Larry: I could do either of those things, I suppose, but finding any qualified replacement would be very hard. Besides, I feel I owe it to Frank to give him every chance to succeed. After all, I did move him along pretty fast.

Bill: So there's an issue of values involved here for you.

Larry: I guess there really is. I just don't think it would be right to fire him—at least right now.

Bill: That's fine. It's just that we need to be clear on what values are involved. Now what I think we should do is take a closer look at the problem itself. I believe you have it all there in the memo. One way of examining the problem more closely would be to answer some questions:

- Who is involved in the problem?
- What exactly is wrong?
- When did the problem first develop?
- Where is the problem taking place?
- Is there a pattern to the problem?

Use the information provided in Larry's memo to answer these five questions. (Note: You may not have enough information to answer all of them, but make an attempt. If you find that you cannot answer a question, list the information that you would need in order to come up with a satisfactory answer.)

1. Who is involved in the problem?

2. What exactly is wrong?

3. When did the problem first develop?

4. Where is the problem taking place?

5. Is there a pattern to the problem?

ACTIVITY 4

☐ As the conversation continues, Bill helps Larry to answer the five questions:

Larry: Well, the answer to the first question is certainly easy. The people involved are Frank and, to a lesser extent, Nancy. And, of course, the customers who are complaining about Frank. But I don't see where this is getting us.

Bill: At this point we can't be sure. But I do know that to solve a problem we need to know what the problem is. These questions can help us figure that out. Is that everyone who's involved?

Larry: I think so.

Bill: How about Frank's wife? Might she be involved in the problem?

Larry: I've thought about that, but as far as I can tell she isn't. At least Frank gives no indication that there's a problem at home.

Bill: Good. But that's something we could find out more about if we needed to?

Larry: Probably. What's the second question?

Bill: What exactly is wrong?

Larry: There are too many customer complaints, and Frank takes too much sick time.

Bill: Anything else?

Larry: I'm having to spend too much time with Nancy. That's part of that secondary objective we identified earlier.

Bill: Right. The third question is "When did the problem first develop?"

Larry: That's a good question. As I remember, not until late this last summer. By the end of August I was certain something was wrong.

Bill: Why do you say that?

Larry: Because by that time Frank had begun taking a lot of sick time, and the customer complaints started coming in just after the Labor Day sale.

Bill: Next question: "Where is the problem taking place?"

Larry: It's taking place in my department—that's where.

Bill: Right. I don't think there is much to help us there. Finally, is there any kind of pattern to the problem? Is it getting worse? Better? Staying about the same?

Larry: It's about the same, although I don't think we've had any complaints about Frank for the last week or so.

Bill: That may be important. We'll see. But at least we have a handle on what the problem actually involves. The next step in solving the problem, however, is sometimes a little tricky. In my experience most problems are caused by some kind of change that has taken place over a period of time. At one point in time there is no problem; then sometime later there's a problem. If we can identify what changed from the time when there was no problem to the time when there was a problem, we can get at the cause.

Larry: That makes sense to me.

Bill: Fine. One way of determining the cause is to compare the problem situation that we have just identified with the same situation at an earlier point in time when the problem did not exist. Can you do that with this problem?

Larry: Sure. Frank started out fine. And then something went wrong. He was even working out well at first as my assistant.

Bill: Then it wasn't Frank's promotion in and of itself that caused the problem?

Larry: Well, that was part of it, but it wasn't the direct cause of the problem.

Bill: All right. If we can agree that a problem is caused by change over time, what is it that has changed from the time Frank was working out fine as your new assistant to the time when the problem was first observed around the end of August?

Given the information provided in Larry's memo, what is your answer to this question? Write your answer in the space that follows.

ACTIVITY 5

☐ Larry continues the conversation by answering Bill's question about what has changed:

Larry: Frank became my assistant in May, and he was working out just fine over the summer. There *were* several changes, but none affected Frank's performance until—that must be it!

Bill: What's that?

Larry: The new fall line, which we brought in during August. That's the only thing that changed from the time when things were going well to the time when the problem became apparent. The other changes might have contributed to the problem, but the new fall line must be the real cause.

Bill: You think that's what caused the problem?

Larry: Sure. Frank had never worked with that merchandise before, and I was too busy spending time with Nancy to break him in.

Bill: It was kind of "sink or swim" for Frank?

Larry: Yes, and I'm afraid he sank. That's got to be it.

Bill: So to come back to our starting point: What are you going to suggest in your meeting tomorrow with Nancy?

If you were Larry, what would be your answer to this question? Write it in the space that follows.

☐ The conversation continues with Larry's answer about what he plans to suggest to Nancy:

Larry: Nothing!

Bill: Nothing? Why's that?

Larry: If the problem is Frank's unfamiliarity with the fall line—and I don't see what else it could be—that's something that should take care of itself in time. And we haven't had any complaints for the last week or so.

Bill: And what about getting Nancy settled into her job?

Larry: I don't think that's going to take too much more time. I should certainly be back in the department full-time before Thanksgiving and before the Christmas rush.

Bill: So you'll be able to help Frank through the rush in a way that you couldn't with the fall line?

Larry: Right. That's it. Then when things settle down after Christmas, I'll send Frank to that training he missed. I really appreciate your time!

Bill: Glad I could help you out.

CONCLUSION

In the problem-solving sequence presented in this chapter, Bill did several things that were helpful:

1. ***He insisted that Larry spell out exactly what would constitute a solution to the problem.*** Notice that Bill would not accept Larry's first statement of what would be happening if the problem were satisfactorily solved ("Frank would be doing his job well. There just wouldn't be any more problems.") Instead, Bill urged Larry to become much more specific in terms of eliminating customer complaints and reducing Frank's sick time.

2. ***Bill helped Larry to bring to the surface an important value issue.*** Frank had been moved along too fast; Larry, to his credit, did not feel it would be fair to let Frank go without at least one more chance. Clear values are often essential for effective problem solving.

3. ***By asking Larry to answer questions about who, what, when, and where, Bill helped both Larry and himself pinpoint the problem.*** In this way they avoided the pitfall of solving a problem and then discovering that the object of the solution was not the real problem.

4. ***Bill helped Larry to identify the most likely cause of the problem.*** The other changes noted in the memo may have contributed to the problem, but the problem itself seems to have been precipitated by the introduction of the new fall line of furniture.

5. ***Once the most likely cause was made clear, Bill helped Larry to generate a plan of action.*** The ultimate solution involves a great deal of commitment from

Larry; it includes assisting Nancy in becoming settled in her job, working closely with Frank during the Christmas rush, and then sending Frank to the training course that was missed.

Bill was very effective in helping Larry to move from a clear articulation of his objectives and values through a precise identification of the problem and its cause to the development of an action plan. In short, the conversation presented in this chapter is quite an improvement over the one presented in Chapter 2. The next step is to learn how to complete the process used in the successful conversation. Your first assignment is to review the entire conversation in this chapter because it will be referred to from time to time and also because it contains much of what is taught in the following chapters. Once you have learned the assumptions and strategies that lie behind Bill's questions, you will have learned the heart of integrated problem management. After you are familiar with the details of this conversation, you will be ready to proceed to Chapter 4.

The Three Dimensions of Better Problem Solving

INTRODUCTION

Usually when confronted with a pressing problem, people attempt to come up with a solution as quickly as they can. That is obviously what Bill did in his first attempt to "help" Larry. Although at times all of us have experienced the gratifying feeling of producing the correct answer right away, we have also all undoubtedly experienced the frustration of repeated trial-and-error attempts that end in failure. At times we think we have developed sound solutions, yet soon find that they do not work. At others times we appear to have solved our immediate problems only to discover that in the long run our "solutions" have created still other problems that are even more difficult to solve.

One approach to problem solving that seems to avoid these pitfalls is to emphasize the specification of desired outcomes. One of the key questions Bill asked had to do with what would be happening if the problem were to be solved. Larry's first reply that he simply wanted Frank to be "working well" was not good enough. What Larry actually wanted was to stop the customer complaints and reduce the amount of sick time Frank was taking. The assumption behind this part of the problem-solving conversation is that problems are often not fully understood, analyzed, or solved because they have not been formulated in terms of clear goals, objectives, or outcomes.

Although the specification of a desired state is essential for effective problem solving, it is also essential that a clear picture be gained of the current state in which the problem is being experienced. In establishing objectives, one runs the risk that they may be unrealistic or that when they are achieved they may result in other, unexpected problems. Furthermore, it is often difficult to establish a realistic objective without first understanding the resources and resistance inherent in the current situation. The questions that Bill asked Larry about who was involved in the problem, what the problem was exactly, when the problem started, and so forth were intended to help both Bill and Larry understand the problem situation.

A problem is not really understood until two distinct, but related, kinds of information have been obtained. The first is information about the current situation: Who is involved in the problem? What exactly is wrong? When did the problem start? Where exactly is the problem taking place? What is the cause of the problem? What resources exist or will be needed to solve the problem? Questions such as these help in defining as precisely as possible all that can be known about the problem.

The second kind of information that must be obtained involves a definition of the characteristics of the desired condition: What exactly would be happening if the problem were solved? What evidence would be used to convince an observer that the problem has, in fact, been solved?

All problem solving involves moving from the current state toward a more desired state, and those states must be defined before a problem can be solved.

THE SITUATION-TARGET-PROPOSAL MODEL

Integrated problem management is based on the Situation-Target-Proposal Model, which enables one to organize information about a problem into three interrelated dimensions:

1. ***The situation dimension, which involves identifying relevant information about the essential features of the current state.*** The situation represents the starting point, the problem that needs to be solved. It includes both facts and opinions about the current state of affairs, as well as predictions about the possibility of change.

2. ***The target dimension, which involves clarifying the desired state or what one wants to accomplish and to avoid.*** The target represents the end point, the termination of the problem-solving process, the desired outcome. Terms commonly used to talk about the target include goals, aims, ends, purposes, and objectives.

3. ***The proposal dimension, which involves developing specific action proposals aimed at changing the current state into the desired state.*** The proposal outlines the path from the situation to the target and defines the plan or strategy to be used to change the way things are into the way one would like them to be.

Achieving a clear understanding of the problem as it currently exists (situation), establishing the desired solution (target), and determining the action to be taken (proposal) are the three keys to becoming a more effective problem solver.

THE DOMAINS OF INFORMATION, VALUES, AND IDEAS

Situation, target, and proposal not only define the three elements of effective problem solving but also identify the three domains within which all human communication takes place: information, values, and ideas. The domain of *information* is entered whenever an attempt is made to find out about the current situation. In seeking information one acts as a researcher, asking questions that can be answered by means of the systematic collection of data. For example, if I want to know if a new product is potentially attractive to a specific group of consumers, I may ask a sample of people from this group whether, or under what conditions, they would buy the product. If the information obtained is valid—that is, if the people from whom I obtained it have been honest and the sample of people selected is representative of the entire group—then I should be able to say with some confidence that I have reported or described a situation that actually exists.

To understand the current situation, one must seek information that is not only valid but also useful. In other words it must relate to the target that one is trying to reach. Thus, if the target concerns increased productivity for a new manufacturing unit, then a market survey would be of little use, even if the information obtained were valid. It is surprising to see how often information is collected that relates only marginally to the problem being faced, especially in organizations.

Many problems can be solved through the systematic collection of valid and useful information. However, if the solution to a problem cannot be found in the information that has been collected, then the problem may involve, at least in part, a target conflict. In this case the person attempting to solve the problem must shift his or her attention from the domain of information to the domain of *values*, which is entered whenever an attempt is made to understand and clarify the target. While research prevails in the domain of information, clarification prevails in the domain of values. Unlike traditional approaches to values, which tend to emphasize either enforcement or modeling, value clarification focuses on the *process* of valuing and on the way in which values come to be. As people become clearer about their values, they begin to select solutions to problems that are more and more consistent with those values. As explained in the previous chapter, an important step in solving Larry's problem with Frank was making it clear that there was a value issue involved: Larry's belief that it would be wrong to fire Frank.

Unfortunately, people are not always clear about their values. Sometimes decisions are made that, on reflection, appear inconsistent with personal or organizational values. A thorough examination of the domain of values helps to ensure that the objectives one is attempting to meet will be more consistently and directly related to one's most important values.

The domain of *ideas* is entered whenever an attempt is made to generate a proposal intended to move from the current to the desired state. More than is the case with either information or values, ideas are sometimes fragile, often misunderstood, and easily lost. Information exists in the world; even though we may ignore or misinterpret it, we can often go back into the world and retrieve it. Similarly, even though values may be ignored or distorted, they resist extinction. If anything, we most often are frustrated by their resistance to change.

Ideas, on the other hand, are easy to lose and difficult to recover. Two processes are essential to the generation and preservation of ideas. One of these processes is *divergence*. People who are being creative in the production of new ideas must at certain times be given the opportunity to be different, to diverge from one another and from the constraints of everyday thought. Divergence requires minimal censorship of ideas, minimal restriction in the opportunity for people to express themselves and take risks, and minimal adherence to traditional rules or procedures for the generation of ideas.

The other process is *convergence*. People must be given the opportunity to build on one another's ideas, to identify areas of similarity in their ideas, and to arrive at some form of agreement about a desired course of action. Convergence requires problem solvers to observe specific rules and procedures, to listen to one another, and to be supportive yet critical of one another's ideas. The domain of ideas often requires a subtle and skillfully managed interplay between convergence and divergence.

CONCLUSION

The dimensions of situation, target, and proposal require problem solvers to enter the domains of information, values, and ideas respectively. These dimensions constitute the interrelated elements of integrated problem management. As shown later in this book, the three dimensions are closely connected; no one dimension should necessarily be addressed before the others. We will proceed for the moment, however, as if problem solving were a linear process moving from the establishment of a target (values) through an understanding of the situation (information) to the generation, selection, and implementation of one or more proposals (ideas). Once this linear process is understood, we can then return to the domains of information, values, and ideas to describe the ways in which they are so closely interrelated.

5

Your Personal Style of Problem Solving

The chapters that follow show you how to make clearer distinctions among situation, target, and proposals and should help you work more effectively with each of these dimensions and in the corresponding domains of information, values, and ideas. Before proceeding, however, it would be a good idea to collect some information about your preferred problem-solving style. Knowing more about the way in which you like to solve problems can help identify your strengths and weaknesses as a problem solver as well as focus your attention on particular aspects of integrated problem management. To learn about your own style, you will need to complete The Problem-Solving Style Inventory, which was designed for this purpose.

The Problem-Solving Style Inventory

Take as much time as you like completing the inventory, but be sure to respond honestly to the items. Do not respond as you think you should or would like to behave, but as you actually behave when solving problems. Feel free to change your responses after further reflection if you wish, but do not be concerned about consistency among responses or certainty. There are no "right" or "wrong" responses.

Each of the ten following items begins with an incomplete sentence, followed by three different sentence completions. Distribute 10 points—no more and no less—among the three endings to show the degree to which each ending describes the way you think or behave. You may use zeros to indicate that a particular alternative is completely unlike you, but use whole numbers only. The following is an example of a completed sentence:

When I find myself facing a complex problem, I tend to:

$\boxed{2}$	Seek help from my friends	$\boxed{8}$	Work out the problem for myself	$\boxed{0}$	Seek professional help

The "Problem-Solving Style Inventory" is adapted from and based on the concepts of Relationship Awareness Theory as presented in the *Strength Deployment Inventory*® by Elias H. Porter, 1973, Pacific Palisades, CA: Personal Strengths Publishing, Inc. Used by permission.

1. I am impressed with other problem solvers who are able to:
   - ☐ Clarify goals and objectives
   - ☐ Offer the best solution
   - ☐ Ask the right questions

2. My definition of effective problem solving includes concern about:
   - ☐ "Having a vision"
   - ☐ Getting the job done
   - ☐ Being "down to earth"

3. I am most satisfied when I am determining:
   - ☐ How things should be
   - ☐ How to make things better
   - ☐ How things are now

4. When I am bothered by something, I tend to focus on:
   - ☐ How I would like things to be different
   - ☐ What I should do to make things better
   - ☐ The cause of the problem

5. When I am under pressure to solve a problem, I am likely to:
   - ☐ Spend time thinking about what I want
   - ☐ Push for a rapid solution to the problem
   - ☐ Step back and carefully examine the situation

6. I am most interested in:
   - ☐ The way things could be
   - ☐ How to improve things
   - ☐ The way things are now

7. When I am working with a group, I tend to help the group:
   - ☐ Determine goals
   - ☐ Take action
   - ☐ Obtain the facts

8. When I find out that another person does not like me or is angry with me, I tend to:
   - ☐ Try to understand what that person wants
   - ☐ Try to make things better between us
   - ☐ Try to find out what is wrong

9. When another person asks me for help with a problem, I tend to:
   - ☐ Find out what that person wants to accomplish
   - ☐ Suggest ways that person could solve the problem
   - ☐ Ask for more information

10. People in general are likely to get into trouble when they:
    - ☐ Lack a vision of what things could be like
    - ☐ Are unwilling to take a few risks
    - ☐ Act without a clear understanding of consequences

The Problem-Solving Style Inventory
Scoring Sheet

Add the numbers you have assigned in each of the three response columns of the inventory (left column, middle column, and right column) and write each column total in the appropriate blank below. The numbers you write in the three blanks below should total 100.

_____ Column 1 (left)

_____ Column 2 (middle)

_____ Column 3 (right)

To adjust your scores so that they can be compared with one another, add 5 points to your score in Column 1, leave your score in Column 2 unchanged, and subtract 5 points from your score in Column 3. Write your adjusted scores in the blanks below.

_____ Column 1 (*Idealist; preference for target and values*)

_____ Column 2 (*Activist; preference for proposals and ideas*)

_____ Column 3 (*Realist; preference for situation and information*)

Now examine the following scale to obtain an estimate of the relative strength of each of your three final scores.

Scale

100-85	Very High
61-84	High
46-60	Above Average
20-45	Average
10-19	Low
0-9	Very Low

Finally, provide the information requested below by listing each of your scores and whether it is high, above average, average, or whatever.

My *Idealist* score of _____ is _____.

My *Activist* score of _____ is _____.

My *Realist* score of _____ is _____.

When attempting to solve problems, different people tend to prefer working with situation, target, or proposals (information, values, or ideas) and, thus, exhibit different problem-solving styles. For example, some people tend to spend a great deal of time and energy being *realists*. They dwell on the current situation and spend most of their time collecting information about the problem. Others tend to be *idealists*. They dwell on the target or how things should be rather than how things are, and they spend most of their time talking about and clarifying values. Still others tend to be *activists*. For these people it is of greatest importance to accomplish things. They spend most of their time creating proposals or generating ideas that they think will solve problems. A fourth group tends to be *pragmatists*. Such people attempt to balance their efforts in the three dimensions and their corresponding domains, spending some time and energy on the situation (collecting information), the target (clarifying values), and proposals (generating ideas).

The Problem-Solving Style Inventory is an attempt to provide you with some information about which aspects of problem solving you prefer. If you have a high score in one problem-solving style and average to low scores in the others, you probably tend to work most comfortably in the style represented by the high score. If two of your scores are fairly close and the third somewhat lower, you probably tend to move back and forth between the two higher styles. If all three of your scores are average, you are probably a pragmatist.

Remember, however, that your scores provide only a rough approximation of the way you go about solving problems. Therefore, as you read the following style descriptions (Porter, 1973), keep in mind not only your scores but also what you know to be true about your usual approach to problems. In this way you will be able to put together a profile for yourself that accurately reflects your problem-solving style.

1. **Realist.** This person is careful, cautious, rational, logical, and analytical. The realist's basic belief is that problems can best be solved by a thorough analysis of the current situation and a clear understanding of the cause or causes of the problem. The realist is reluctant to take any action until he or she clearly understands what actually is happening. Above all, the realist wants to avoid what he or she sees as the wishful thinking of the idealist and the unanticipated consequences so often produced by the activist.

The realist's greatest strength is the ability to collect information and to ask hard questions about the problem situation. His or her greatest weakness, however, is the tendency toward "analysis paralysis." The realist can never obtain enough information and consequently may continue to collect data long after there is a need to do so, never moving into action. At the extreme, the realist may become so immersed in information that he or she becomes almost invested in the status quo. "That's the way things are," the realist may seem to say. "You'll never change them."

2. **Idealist.** Unlike the realist, the idealist sees things not as they are but as they might be. He or she tends to be visionary, hopeful, trusting, and future oriented. The idealist's basic belief is that problem solving can be successful only if people have a clear sense of their values, of what they want and where they are going. Above all, the idealist wants to avoid what he or she sees as the mundane, pedestrian thinking of the realist and the hasty decision making of the activist.

The strength of the idealist is his or her ability to challenge the sometimes-limited thinking of the realist and to provide new perspectives on old problems for the activist. The weakness of the idealist is his or her frequent dissatisfaction. The confirmed idealist is someone who can pick out the flaw in any situation. Within minutes of arriving on a new job, entering a new relationship, or purchasing a new car or home, the idealist is imagining how things could be improved. Instead of accepting what must be accepted, the idealist tries to create utopias. Like the realist, but for quite different reasons, the idealist too often fails to act.

3. *Activist.* The activist wants to accomplish things immediately. He or she tends to be energetic, confident, and enterprising. The activist's basic belief is that problems can be solved only by generating proposals and ideas, by making something happen. Above all, the activist wants to avoid what he or she sees as the realist's tendency to analyze the obvious and the hopelessly romantic thinking of the idealist.

The strength of the activist is his or her ability to move into action, to do something that may solve the problem. Like the idealist, the activist charges the realist with a lack of courage and vision. Like the realist, the activist confronts the idealist with the limitations of utopian thinking. From the activist's point of view, the problem with both realists and idealists is an unwillingness to take risks. That risk taking, however, is the activist's greatest weakness. In an overeagerness to take action, the activist may do almost anything and thus make the problem situation even worse. The activist is the ultimate trial-and-error problem solver.

4. *Pragmatist.* This person tends to use a style that combines the three just described, shifting from dimension to dimension depending on the demands of the problem. Pragmatists tend to pride themselves on being flexible, adaptable, responsive, and tolerant. Their basic belief is that the appropriate response to a problem depends on a number of variables. When confronted with a new problem, pragmatists tend to become realists by concentrating on the situation and collecting needed information. When confronted with an old, unchanging problem, they tend to become idealists, concerning themselves with values and creating images of how things might be changed. And when confronted with the press of time, they tend to become activists, coming up with proposals and ideas to meet the challenge of the moment. Above all, pragmatists want to avoid collecting information for its own sake (extreme realist behavior), excessive daydreaming (extreme idealist behavior), and unnecessary risk taking (extreme activist behavior).

The obvious strength of the pragmatist is flexibility. Sometimes it is important to keep one's options open and not to commit oneself to a particular approach. However, this stance also has disadvantages. Because the pragmatist is so committed to being flexible and so dependent on his or her ability to read the problem correctly, the pragmatist may use one of the three other styles at the wrong time and thus produce many of the same destructive outcomes associated with the more extreme behaviors that he or she is actually trying to avoid. Finally, because of his or her tendency to move from dimension to dimension, the pragmatist may be perceived by others as unpredictable.

Your scores on The Problem-Solving Style Inventory help to indicate which of these four styles is most characteristic of you. The chances are that you will prefer to work in the style in which your scores are high and to avoid styles in which your scores are low. The good news is that you probably have a great deal of experience working in your preferred problem-solving style and that you will be most comfortable with the parts of this book that deal with that style and the associated dimension of the problem-solving process.

The bad news, however, is even more interesting. First, simply because you prefer to use a particular style and work in a particular dimension does not necessarily mean that you are good at doing so. It may be that you have never given much thought to how you actually go about using your preferred style. Second, you will probably find those parts of this book that deal with dimensions in which you have fairly low scores less interesting and less comfortable. For instance, when an activist reads the next chapter on identifying the target, which is the preferred dimension of the idealist, he or she may feel restless (as activists often do) and may want to proceed to the more "interesting" parts of the book—that is, the parts with which he or she would be most comfortable. All of us, consequently, have something to learn from an examination of those dimensions we are most familiar with as well as from studying those dimensions in which we have the least experience.

The following chapters present you with specific ideas and strategies for working with the dimensions of situation, target, and proposal. Two cautions are offered before we proceed:

1. *Only rarely does a problem require extensive analysis of all three dimensions.* Some problems, for example, are largely situational; if the people involved can come to a clear understanding of the current situation, the solution becomes obvious. Other problems are more value related; once those involved become clearly aware of what the target actually is, they can move into action. Still other problems are largely a matter of proposals; those involved know what the situation is and what they want, but they do not know what to do to reach the desired state. In each of these cases it would be best to work primarily with the dimension mostly closely related to the problem at hand. Devoting extensive time and attention to the other dimensions would be a waste.

2. *For each of the dimensions we provide you with a series of specific steps; but these steps are intended only as guidelines for problem solving, not as a rigid sequence to be worked through each time a problem arises.* A single substep, for instance, may be all that you need to clarify your thinking on a particular issue. In that case complete the substep and ignore the rest of the process. Problem solving is not meant to be a career, only a tool to help you manage your personal and professional concerns more effectively.

REFERENCE

Porter, E.H. (1973). *Strength deployment inventory® manual of administration and interpretation.* Pacific Palisades, CA: Personal Strengths Publishing, Inc.

6

Identifying the Target

One of the major strengths of the Situation-Target-Proposal Model is its flexibility. It is often possible to start anywhere in the model and move in any direction; it is even possible to work in all three dimensions at the same time. For the purpose of learning the model, however, it is best to start with the *target* dimension. If people do not know where they are going, they are likely to be surprised or unhappy about the end point. In some cases, of course, a target analysis is unnecessary. If your car will not start, for example, the target is obvious: You want the car to start.

In other cases, however, the problem may involve more complex issues. Once the car is running, should it be kept or traded for another car? A number of problems may involve a subtle interplay of values, a complex interaction of possible objectives. In such a case an identification of the target is essential. The following steps are useful in target identification.

STEP 1: IDENTIFY GOALS

In the furniture-store example used earlier, Bill and Larry were trying to figure out what to do about Frank. Early in their successful problem-solving conversation, Bill suggested that Larry describe what would be happening if the problem were satisfactorily solved. When you are attempting to identify the target in a problem-solving endeavor of your own, you need to follow Bill's example and begin by determining what the situation would look like if the problem were solved. Ask questions such as the following:

- What would look different?
- What would feel different?
- What would be different?
- When is this happening?
- Where is it happening?

However, as you will recall, Larry's first response to Bill's question was that he wanted Frank to be "doing his job well." This initial response was not specific, and Bill followed it by asking Larry to provide a more concrete statement of what he wanted.

Consequently, once you have created a scenario of the future, examine that scenario for the goals that are implicit in it. Ask questions such as these:

- How would I know that the desired state had occurred?
- What would be the benchmarks of my success?
- How could I prove to someone else that the problem had been successfully solved?

In response to Bill's encouragement, Larry acknowledged his desire to eliminate customer complaints and to reduce the amount of sick time Frank was taking. However, these were only the most important of Larry's goals in this situation. He also wanted to see to it that Nancy, his new boss, was settled into her job; he wanted to return to his department full-time; and, at least by implication, he wanted Frank to be better trained for his job. Most problems of any consequence have more than one goal, and identifying those goals is essential.

STEP 2: COMPARE GOALS WITH VALUES

The target lies in the domain of values; and when you are involved in a problem-solving effort, the goals you have identified should reflect your values. As suggested in Chapter 4, however, few people are always certain about what their values actually are. Far too often people tend to make decisions that they later discover are inconsistent with important personal or organizational values. To keep this from happening, you need to compare the goals that you have developed in Step 1 with some clearly articulated set of values that you have taken the time to establish and record in written form.

If the problem you are attempting to solve involves organizational values, you must be certain that the goals you have established are consistent with the organization's values. Some companies articulate their values and make them known to employees, which makes it possible for an individual employee to compare his or her problem-solving goals with those values; others have not written and published their values. If you work for a company that has not made its values known, you may wish to refer the appropriate people in the company to such books as Ouchi's (1981) *Theory Z: How American Business Can Meet the Japanese Challenge*, Pascale and Athos's (1982) *The Art of Japanese Management: Applications for American Executives*, and Peters and Waterman's (1982) *In Search of Excellence: Lessons from America's Best Run Companies*, all of which argue for the importance of articulating corporate values and provide guidelines and examples for doing so.

However, you can do something right now about your own personal values. The following activities help you to clarify and record them so that in your future problem-solving efforts you will be able to compare your goals and actions with your recorded values.

Life-Values Assessment[4]

Listed below are fifteen life values. Quickly set their priorities, ranking them from 1 to 15 in terms of their importance to you (1 = most important; 15 = least important). Write each value's priority in the blank to the left.

_____ Affection   To obtain and share companionship and affection

_____ Duty   To dedicate myself to what I call duty

_____ Expertise   To become an authority

_____ Family   To have a close relationship with my family

_____ Independence   To have freedom of thought and action

_____ Leadership   To be influential

_____ Parenthood   To raise, nurture, and support my children

_____ Personal Growth   To optimize my personal development

_____ Pleasure   To enjoy life

_____ Power   To have control over others

_____ Prestige   To become well known

_____ Religion   To be consistent with religious values

_____ Security   To be stable and secure

_____ Service   To contribute to others

_____ Wealth   To have a great deal of money

---

[4]Based on an activity presented in *A Life Planning Workbook* (p. 10) by G.A. Ford and G.L. Lippitt, 1972, Fairfax, Virginia: NTL Learning Resources Corporation. Adapted by permission of NTL Institute.

Once you have established priorities, begin eliminating your lowest-ranked values. Cross out your fifteenth-ranked value, then your fourteenth, then your thirteenth. Continue working your way through the list until you find that you cannot cross out any more values because life, as you define it, would begin to lose much of its meaning if you could not live the remaining values. In doing this, if you find that you want to rerank certain items, do so. When you have finished, proceed to the next activity.

Career-Values Assessment[5]

Without referring to the list that you have just completed, go through the same process with the following list of career values. Set their priorities, ranking them from 1 to 15; then eliminate as many of the lower-ranked values as possible.

_____	Adventure	To experience risky and exciting situations
_____	Challenge	To meet new and unusual problems
_____	Creativity	To produce new and unusual work
_____	Independence	To direct my own career
_____	Leadership	To direct and influence others
_____	Mastery	To reach a high level of skill
_____	Money	To earn a high income
_____	Moral Value	To be consistent with a moral code
_____	People	To work closely with others
_____	Quality	To produce work of the highest possible excellence
_____	Recognition	To have my work known and respected
_____	Security	To establish a secure career

---

[5]Based on an activity presented in *A Life Planning Workbook* (p. 10) by G. A. Ford and G. L. Lippitt, 1972, Fairfax, Virginia: NTL Learning Resources Corporation. Adapted by permission of NTL Institute.

_____ Self-Expression   To express my personality in my work

_____ Service   To have my career benefit others

_____ Variety   To try new and different things

Next compare the values that remain on your two completed lists. Some people find these two lists quite compatible, while others find certain conflicts between them. If you find such a conflict, you may want to begin thinking about ways of resolving or negotiating that difference. Then examine the two lists, adding any values that are important to you that do not appear on either list. (Innovation, excellence, truth, financial security, and integrity are a few that some people consider adding.) Finally, reduce what you have to a list of your ten core or most important values and record them here.

1. _____

2. _____

3. _____

4. _____

5. _____

6. _____

7. _____

8. _____

9. _____

10. _____

At this point some people like to rank order their final lists to establish a sense of the relative importance of each value and even to expand the definitions of their values so that they know exactly what those values mean to them. If you would like to do this, we encourage you to do so. Even if you do not, however, you have taken important action toward making values a consistent part of your goal setting because you have produced a clearly articulated set of values against which you can compare any goals identified in a problem-solving effort.

STEP 3: PLACE GOALS ON A TARGET

By now in your reading you may have wondered why we have used the word "target" in talking about goals. There is a difference between goals and target, and this difference is one of the most important things we have learned about problem solving. Complex problems have multiple goals, and those goals are almost always related to one another. The concept of the target allows people to understand that relationship more clearly.

A target, as it is usually understood (see Figure 1), consists of a series of concentric rings around a bull's-eye. Usually the inner rings are considered of greater value than the outer rings. The bull's-eye is considered to be of greatest value. When you are trying to solve a problem, think of a target and identify the bull's-eye: the central value or goal that you want to accomplish. Then locate other values and goals at various distances from the bull's-eye, placing each in its own separate ring. Those that are of considerable importance should be placed in the inner rings of the target, closer to the bull's-eye; those that are of less importance should be placed in the outer rings. In other words, the proximity of goals to the bull's-eye reflects the relative importance of each goal.

The relationship of each goal to the bull's-eye, however, represents only one of two dimensions of the target. The other dimension is the spatial relationship that exists among the goals themselves.

Given unlimited resources, you could probably accomplish all of the goals on your target. Often, however, your resources will not be unlimited; and you will need to direct your efforts toward the accomplishment of certain goals at the expense of others. Like most people, you probably do that by directing more attention to those goals that are close to the bull's-eye.

An examination of the relationship among the goals sometimes may cause you to take a different approach. Begin by placing your goals on a target as just described. Place the most important goal in the bull's-eye, the next-most important in the next ring, and so forth. Then examine each of the goals by asking "Would my investment of energy in accomplishing this goal have a positive, negative, or neutral impact on

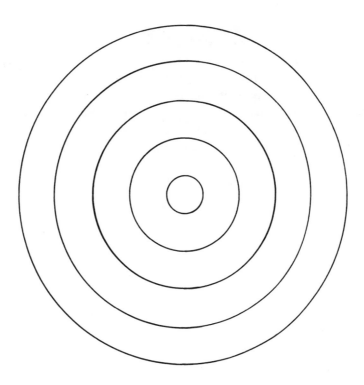

Figure 1. Target Illustration

the accomplishment of the other goals?'' Simply move each goal around the target, keeping it in the same ring, but moving it close to other goals that are similar or compatible and away from goals that are different or incompatible.

In the case study involving Larry's problem with Frank Foster, a rank ordering of Larry's goals according to priority might look like this:

1. Eliminate customer complaints about Frank.
2. Reduce Frank's sick time.
3. See that Nancy is settled into her new job.
4. Get Larry back to his department full-time.
5. Ensure that Frank is better trained for his job.

To practice using a target for problem solving, complete the empty target in Figure 2 to assist in solving Larry's problem; use a pencil so that you can erase easily. First place each of the five goals in the appropriate place on the target; Goal 1 goes in the bull's-eye, Goal 2 in the next ring, and so forth. Next, keeping the goals in their assigned rings, move each goal close to other goals that are similar or compatible and away from goals that are quite different or incompatible. Compare goals with each other, mentally answering the question "If I were to invest my resources in accomplishing this goal, would I be more or less likely to achieve this other goal?"

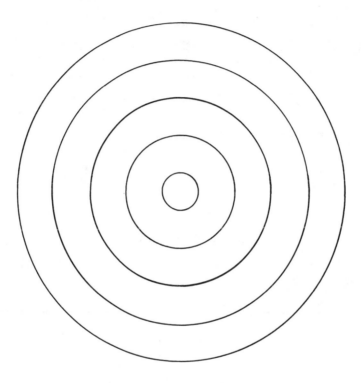

Goal 1: Eliminate customer complaints about Frank.

Goal 2: Reduce Frank's sick time.

Goal 3: See that Nancy is settled into her new job.

Goal 4: Get Larry back to his department full-time.

Goal 5: Ensure that Frank is better trained for his job.

Figure 2. Practice Target for Larry's Problem

When you have completed your target, compare it with the one illustrated in Figure 3. In this target Goal 1 is in the bull's-eye, and Goal 2 is in the next ring. These two are kept close together because of their obviously close relationship. Goal 3 is placed in the third ring but is moved opposite Goals 1 and 2 because the time that Larry would need to invest in settling Nancy into her job would be in conflict with improving Frank's work. Goal 4, however, although less important than Goal 3, is closely related to Goals 1 and 2 because if Larry were to return to his department full-time he could work more closely with Frank. Goal 4 is opposed to Goal 3 because spending time settling Nancy into her job would hinder the possibility of getting Larry back to his department. Goal 5, the least important, is placed in the outside ring, seems unrelated to the other four, and is thus located apart from them.

Three interesting insights emerge from this analysis:

1. Goals 1, 2, and 4 constitute a cluster and might well be addressed at the same time.

2. Goal 3, which is opposed to the two most central goals as well as to Goal 4, may be what we call an "enabling goal": It is a lower-priority goal, but its accomplishment might make the achievement of other, higher-priority goals more likely. If Larry could expedite or complete the process of settling Nancy into her job, he would then have time to accomplish his two most important goals as well as Goal 4.

3. Goal 5 is both least important and unrelated to the other goals. Its accomplishment can wait until later.

When working in the target dimension, keep in mind that you are working with values and that consequently there is no right or wrong way to complete any of these steps. Priorities reflect values, and the best you can do is to be as clear about your values as possible. However, priorities are sometimes difficult to establish, especially for a group; when you are involved in a group problem-solving effort, you may wish to refer to "Setting Priorities" in the Appendix of this book. In those cases in which the exact relationship among goals is not clear or easily understood, the discussion of what we call a "cross-impact analysis" (see the Appendix) may also be helpful.

As you have been reading this chapter, you have probably thought of a problem that would lend itself to this kind of process. To further practice working with a target, ask yourself what the situation would look like if this problem were solved. Write your response in the space that follows.

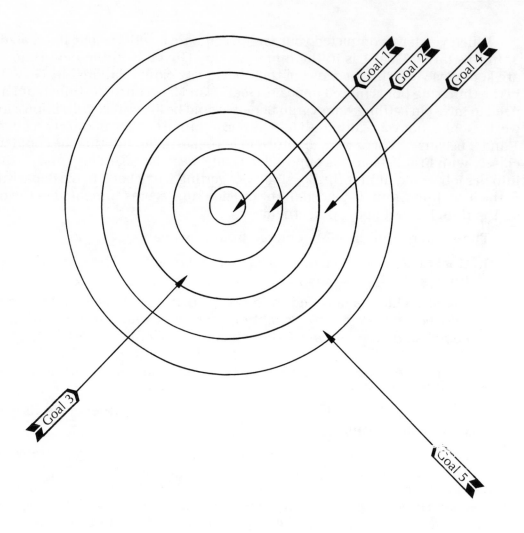

Goal 1: Eliminate customer complaints about Frank.

Goal 2: Reduce Frank's sick time.

Goal 3: See that Nancy is settled into her new job.

Goal 4: Get Larry back to his department full-time.

Goal 5: Ensure that Frank is better trained for his job.

Figure 3. Suggested Target Completion for Larry's Problem

Next examine your response on page 39 for the goals implicit in it. Ask yourself what specifically would need to happen to allow you to demonstrate to someone else that the problem had been solved. Write at least four or five different goals in the space that follows; then set their priorities by ranking them (writing 1 next to the highest-priority goal, 2 next to the second highest, and so forth). To establish these priorities, ask yourself which of the goals you *must* accomplish to solve the problem and which you would only *like to* accomplish.

Finally, place these goals on the target illustration in Figure 4, with those that are related to one another on one side and those that are opposed on the other. Then mentally answer the following questions:

1. Which of these goals cluster together and might be addressed at the same time?

2. Are there any enabling goals (lower-priority goals that, when accomplished, would help to achieve other, higher-priority goals)?

3. Are there any low-priority goals that are clearly unrelated to any of the others and that can be put on hold, at least for now?

After answering these questions, complete the target illustration.

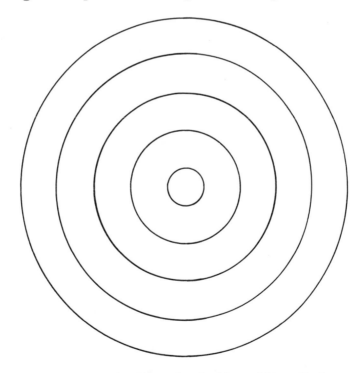

Figure 4. Practice Target for Problem of Your Choice

By conceiving of goals as clustered on a target, one can gain an appreciation for the subtle and often important interrelationships among goals. Most "real-life" problems are too complex to be described by a single goal or by a list of goals that are not in some sense interrelated. You have made important progress toward solving a problem when you can specify several goals and values that cluster together on a target and you can describe the interrelationships among them.

REFERENCES

Ford, G.A., & Lippitt, G.L. (1972). *A life planning workbook.* Fairfax, VA: NTL Learning Resources Corporation.

Ouchi, W. (1981). *Theory Z: How American business can meet the Japanese challenge.* Reading, MA: Addison-Wesley.

Pascale, R.T., & Athos, A.G. (1982). *The art of Japanese management: Applications for American executives.* New York: Warner.

Peters, T.J., & Waterman, R.H., Jr. (1982). *In search of excellence: Lessons from America's best run companies.* New York: Harper & Row.

7

Assessing the Situation

Very early in this book we suggested that the error most people make in problem solving is jumping from an initial awareness of the problem to a series of trial-and-error solutions, most of which fail to correct the situation and may, in fact, make the problem worse. This tendency is particularly true for people with even moderately high activist scores on The Problem-Solving Style Inventory. Although the urge to "do something" is often strong, it is important to resist that urge and first assess the situation and determine the target.

A proposal is an attempt to move from the current situation to the target, from where one is to where one wants to go. In the previous chapter we made some suggestions about how to clarify the target. This chapter focuses on the problem situation itself. Although we could have begun with an analysis of the situation before moving to the target, we have frequently found that a clear target helps to guide our work in understanding the situation. Some people, particularly those with high "realist" scores, have a tendency to collect more information than they really need. By understanding where they want to go, they have a better chance of collecting information that is relevant to the identified target.

Another way of helping to ensure that the information collected will be relevant to the problem at hand is to concentrate on the six categories of information that are most likely to prove useful in understanding the problem situation. These categories have to do with *who* is involved in the problem, *what* specifically is wrong, *where* exactly the problem is occurring, *when* the problem occurs (or at least when it was first observed), and what the *extent* and the *pattern* of the problem are. You will remember that when we were dealing with Larry's problem, Bill asked Larry to answer a series of questions based on these categories; in this way Bill was able to help both himself and Larry come to a fuller understanding of the problem situation.

Sometimes, of course, in exploring these six categories, people discover that they do not have answers to all of the questions. However, by going through the process, they at least generate what we call "researchable questions." A researchable question is one that has a verifiable answer. The question "Should Frank have been sent to the training program provided by his company?" is not such a question since people may very well have different opinions on that matter. The question "Has Frank's rate of absenteeism exceeded the company average?" is researchable since it should be possible to collect information on this subject that everyone involved can agree is accurate.

STEP 1: IDENTIFY RELEVANT SITUATIONAL INFORMATION

If there is anything we would like you to learn from this chapter, it is the terms *who, what, where, when, extent,* and *pattern.* When attempting to solve a problem, your responses to key questions in these six categories will provide all of the information that can be known about the situation.

The first two terms, *who* and *what,* are fairly self-explanatory: Who is involved in the problem? What exactly is wrong? The other four terms, however, are sometimes a bit tricky. *Where* obviously has to do with where the problem is taking place. This could be defined in a strictly geographical sense (the east coast, southern California, a small town in upstate New York); or it might refer to a particular production line, department, or even management level. But in those problems involving a physical object, you might also want to ask where *on the defective object* the problem is taking place. In the next chapter, for example, we will look at a case study involving a one-half-inch gouge on some wooden tabletops. The fact that the gouge always occurs in the same place on each tabletop rather than on random places is important in understanding the problem.

When has to do with *when the problem began* and sometimes *when the problem was first observed.* For instance, in Larry's problem with Frank, the problem was taking place in a particular department; and it began at about the end of August. However, on other occasions, as is the case with the problem featured in the next chapter, all that can be determined at first is when the problem was originally observed.

Finally, the questions connected with *extent* and *pattern* sometimes provide different answers depending on the problem situation. *Extent* is spatial and has to do with how widespread the problem is. *Pattern,* on the other hand, is concerned with how the problem is changing or has changed over time: Is it becoming better or worse, staying the same, or varying in some systematic or erratic way? In the case of Larry's problem with Frank, the extent of the problem was largely focused in the furniture department. As far as the pattern was concerned, in view of the fact that no customer complaints had been made about Frank in the last week before Larry spoke with Bill, the problem seemed to be getting better.

Thus, the key questions to ask in a problem situation are as follows:

- Who is involved in the problem?
- What exactly is wrong?
- Where is the problem taking place? (In what location and/or where on the defective object is it taking place?)
- When did the problem begin (and/or when was the problem first observed)?
- What is the extent of the problem?
- What is the pattern of the problem?

When working with these questions, you may wish to record your answers on a form such as that illustrated in Figure 5. For a lengthy list of similar questions that you might like to consider, see "Fifty Questions" in the Appendix of this book.

Remember that not every question will work with every problem. The question "Where on the defective object is the problem taking place?" obviously would not be appropriate in the case of Larry's problem with Frank. The answers to those questions that are appropriate to the problem at hand, however, will give you all of the information that you need about the problem situation.

	Information About Current Situation
Who	
What	
Where	
When	
Extent	
Pattern	

Figure 5. Form for Analyzing Current Situation

STEP 2: IDENTIFY THE SOURCES OF INFORMATION

In most situations the sources of information about the problem are fairly obvious, and all you need to do is proceed with the job of collecting that information. You may be working alone or perhaps at best with one other person, and you may have very little time or money available for information collection. In such cases the best approach is to ask yourself what is known about the problem in the six categories of *who, what, where, when, extent,* and *pattern*. In other, more complex situations, you may have the time, money, or other resources you need to collect more information about the situation. In these cases you may wish to give some attention to various sources of information such as those outlined in "Five Ways to Obtain Information" in the Appendix of this book.

STEP 3: COLLECT THE NEEDED INFORMATION

The only word of warning here is that you should attempt to collect the needed information in such a way that you influence that information as little as possible. This may sound easier than it actually is. Observing someone doing a job may affect the way in which that person does the job. Interviewing him or her about how the job is done and *then* observing may even further affect the way in which the job is performed. Although subjective sources of information may need to be used, be aware of the possible effect your information collection may have on the accuracy of the information itself.

Once you have collected the needed information, summarize and categorize it in terms of *who, what, where, when, extent,* and *pattern.* At this point you should have a reasonably full understanding of the problem situation and be ready to move on either to an identification of the cause of the problem and the resources available to solve it (Chapter 8) or to the development of one or more proposals to move you from where you are now to where you want to be (Chapter 9). However, before we proceed to these next two phases, we would like to review the problem-solving process as it has been presented thus far by taking at look at a case study that we frequently use in our workshops.

The Case of King Printing Corporation

☐ King Printing Corporation is a rapidly growing firm located in a medium-sized western city. As president you are faced with making a personnel decision that will have a significant impact on the future of your company.

You began King Printing about ten years ago as a one-person shop operating on money from a second mortgage on your house. About two years later the city, which was small at that time, experienced a phenomenal period of growth and development. Several major electronics firms moved into the area, and the local teachers' college was expanded into a fairly large state university. You were able to land contracts with most of these new enterprises, providing them not only with routine printing needs (stationery, forms, and so forth) but also with extensive advertising and promotional materials. Your company now prints the university catalog and most of the materials used by the university for external promotion.

As a result of this work and of business that developed from it throughout the region, King Printing is now a major corporation in the state. You are no longer involved in the day-to-day operation of the company, but instead spend your time developing new clients and contacts throughout the West. You are also beginning to play a role at the state level in establishing guidelines for vocational education. You are finding this very enjoyable, although it is cutting into the time that you are able to devote to the company.

To handle the daily business concerns, several years ago you hired a vice president, Joe Clark. Joe was something of a find for you since he had considerable experience in the printing industry as the owner of his own small printing company back East. Joe, however, was unhappy with the large urban area where he was located. The position you were able to offer him, which included stock options, plus your western location were just too much for him to resist. Joe is fifty-seven years old now and has done an excellent job for you. Although he is hard driving and believes in supervising his managers quite closely, he has earned the respect of everyone in your company as competent, committed, and knowledgeable. Your relationship with him is businesslike, not personal or especially comfortable.

The current organizational structure of King Printing Corporation is as presented in Figure 6. During the last couple of years, as the company has continued to grow, it has become more and more obvious that Joe's close management style and his unwillingness to delegate are increasing the routine administrative paperwork that he feels required to handle personally. This problem has worsened to the point that Joe is beginning to let his overall responsibilities for coordination and planning slide. In response to this development, you are considering creating a fifth managerial position, that of administrative manager. You need someone who can work collaboratively with the other four managers in coordinating and consolidating all of the administrative paperwork of the company while receiving only general policy guidance from Joe. You have discussed this strategy with Joe, and he likes your idea.

What you have not discussed with him is his eventual retirement. Although Joe is still a few years from retirement, you need to plan for the day when Joe will step aside for a younger person. For a variety of reasons, you are not happy with any of your current four managers as candidates for Joe's position; your hope, although you have not expressed it to Joe, is that the person you hire as administrative manager will gain such a complete understanding of the company that he or she will be able to take Joe's place when the time comes.

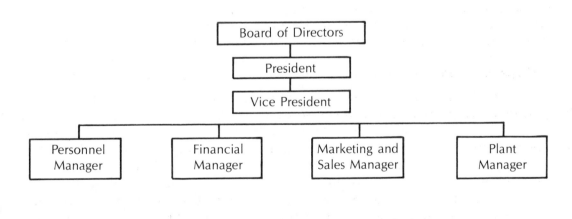

**Figure 6. Organizational Structure
of King Printing Corporation**

Begin solving this problem by determining what you want to accomplish. As you learned in the last chapter, the first step in identifying the target is to develop an image of the future. Before reading on, take a moment to review this case study and use the space that follows to jot down a few notes to yourself about what you would like to see as the situation at King Printing Corporation in a year.

If you are like most of the people who have participated in our workshops, the situation you have envisioned for King Printing Corporation is similar to this:

> In a year the company would have successfully created the new position of administrative manager. That person would be working effectively with Joe and the other managers, and he or she would have the administrative-paperwork problem under control so that Joe would no longer be bothered with it. The new manager would also be well on his or her way to learning the whole business and would need perhaps only three to five years more to be ready to take over for Joe.

When we begin to discuss a scenario like this in our workshops, however, almost always one of the participants will say something like "Wait a minute. That sounds just fine *only if we accept the president's proposal to create a new position.* What we've done is come up with a proposal without going through the kind of analysis we are learning here. What I want to know is what the future might look like if we put aside for the moment the president's proposal to create a new position."

This comment usually creates some disagreement because by that time most of the participants have developed a commitment to creating the new position. Gradually, however, most participants come to see that they have fallen into the same trap as the president. By grabbing at the first solution available, they have jumped over both target and situation.

This is a very important point: The target must be specific enough to provide a sense of direction for a problem-solving effort, yet general enough to allow for the development of a variety of proposals. To include in the target the statement that in a year "the company would have successfully created the new position of administrative manager" allows only one course of action, to create that position. It is crucial to define a future in which the problem is solved *without* at the same time adopting any particular proposal.

Once this principle has been established in the workshop, the participants develop a new version such as this:

> In a year the administrative-paperwork problem would be under control, and some decision would have been made about what the company will do when Joe retires. Other goals are also relevant: A better relationship would exist between Joe and the president, and some of the president's concerns about the other four managers would be resolved. Then the company would be operating in such a way as to allow the president to remain uninvolved in the daily operation so that he could continue both to develop new business around the state and to continue working on establishing vocational-education guidelines.

Next the participants examine this image for the goals implied in it and usually come up with something like the following:

- Handle the administrative-paperwork problem;
- Decide what to do when Joe retires;
- Resolve the president's reservations about the other four managers;
- Keep the president uninvolved in day-to-day operations;
- Allow the president to continue developing new clients in the region;
- Allow the president to continue working on establishing vocational-education guidelines; and
- Establish better relations between Joe and the president.

As we pointed out in the last chapter, there is no "right" way to deal with values. Sometimes different participant groups come up with lists that are slightly different from this one. In general, however, once people begin to explore what would be happening if this problem were solved, they come up with a number of important goals that go well beyond taking care of the administrative paperwork.

The next task is to establish priorities among these goals. This activity frequently generates considerable discussion in our workshops, but a list like the following usually meets with general agreement:

1. Handle the administrative-paperwork problem.
2. Establish better relations between Joe and the president.
3. Decide what to do when Joe retires.
4. Resolve the president's reservations about the other four managers.
5. Keep the president uninvolved in day-to-day operations.
6. Allow the president to continue developing new clients in the region.
7. Allow the president to continue working on establishing vocational-education guidelines.

Finally, these seven priorities are placed on a target like the one presented in Figure 7. Goal 1 is in the bull's-eye, while Goals 2, 3, and 4 cluster together in the next three

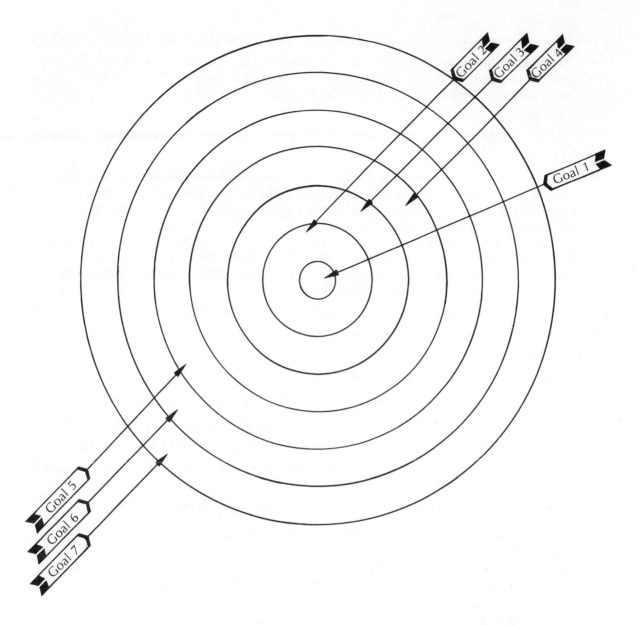

Goal 1: Handle the administrative-paperwork problem.

Goal 2: Establish better relations between Joe and the president.

Goal 3: Decide what to do when Joe retires.

Goal 4: Resolve the president's reservations about the other four managers.

Goal 5: Keep the president uninvolved in day-to-day operations.

Goal 6: Allow the president to continue developing new clients in the region.

Goal 7: Allow the president to continue working on establishing vocational-education guidelines.

**Figure 7. Target Illustration
for Problem at King Printing Corporation**

rings. These three goals relate to the interpersonal or management-development part of the problem but are not directly related to the administrative-paperwork issue. This configuration suggests, by the way, that in solving this problem one could either address the highest priority directly or first go after the next three as a kind of "enabling" cluster of goals, the accomplishment of which would facilitate the accomplishment of Goal 1. Finally, Goals 5, 6, and 7 also cluster together but are opposed to the first four goals, which would seem to require some involvement on the part of the president, at least for a time.

This identification of the target is usually enough to convince most participants in our workshops that the president's original proposal, while still certainly a possibility, fails to address some of the most important goals implied in our vision of the future. This process of disenchantment with the president's original plan continues when we ask participants to analyze the current problem situation. Stop at this point and use the space that follows to write your own answers to these key questions.

1. Who is involved in the problem?

2. What exactly is wrong?

3. Where is the problem taking place?

4. When did the problem begin?

5. What is the extent of the problem?

6. What is the pattern of the problem?

Here are the answers that our participants usually generate:

1. ***Who is involved in the problem?*** Answer: If the problem is defined as handling the increased administrative paperwork, then perhaps only the president and Joe are involved. But the established image of the future implies a number of related problems. If the situation is examined in that light, the other four managers must also be included.

2. ***What exactly is wrong?*** Answer: First, the company has experienced a significant increase in administrative paperwork that Joe will not delegate and for which he was not hired. Nothing is known about the exact nature of this work. Second, no one has been identified to replace Joe when he retires. There is no information about Joe's retirement plans. Third, the president sees something wrong with the other four managers as possible replacements for Joe.

3. ***Where is the problem taking place?*** Answer: It is occurring at King Printing Corporation, which is located in a medium-sized western city.

4. ***When did the problem begin?*** Answer: The paperwork problem began during the last couple of years. There is no information about the management and interpersonal problems, although they seem to have existed for some time.

5. ***What is the extent of the problem?*** Answer: The administrative-paperwork problem seems to be confined to middle and upper management.

6. ***What is the pattern of the problem?*** Answer: The paperwork problem seems to be increasing. There is no information about the pattern of the management or interpersonal problems.

Generally, this analysis of the situation continues to raise reservations about the president's idea of establishing a new management position. It also implies a number of "researchable questions" about the current situation:

- What kind of increased paperwork has caused the problem?
- When is Joe planning to retire?

- What are the president's concerns about the other four managers?
- What exactly is the nature of the president's relationships with Joe and with the other four managers?
- What is the president's management style?

These questions and a number of others may have occurred to you as you worked through your own analysis. The questions that arise indicate that some important things have been learned about problem solving so far:

- The first solution, even though it may appear to be a very good one, may not move you very far toward the real target.
- The problem that originally presents itself may not be the real problem or may be only part of the real problem.
- In responding to questions in the categories of *who, what, where, when, extent,* and *pattern,* you may discover that you know less about the problem than you at first thought.

A clear identification of the target and a thorough understanding of the situation are crucial in the problem-solving process. Before moving on to generating proposals, however, in the next chapter we will deal with the fascinating process of discovering the cause of a problem.

Establishing Causes and Resources

We have already suggested that integrated problem management is not composed of a rigid series of steps that must be slavishly followed with every problem. Instead, our intention is to present an approach to problem solving that offers a variety of tools and strategies that can be used as needed. This view of integrated problem management is particularly relevant for the material covered in this chapter.

Some problems have clear and obvious causes. In such cases it is foolish to spend time analyzing the obvious; instead, the people involved should move directly to developing one or more proposals. Similarly, in some situations people have all the resources necessary for problem solving and they need spend little or no time worrying about resources. But on other occasions a problem may have a single, unknown cause or a series of multiple and perhaps highly interactive causes. Also, at times people are not sure about what resources they have or what to do in view of the fact that resources are limited. In instances such as these last two, the process of *causal/resource analysis,* which is outlined in this chapter, can be used to help in developing an understanding of complex or unknown causes and in clarifying actual or potential resources.

The following case study offers a simple situation to illustrate how to determine an unknown cause.

The Dead-Car Case

☐ John and Jane Hill are a young married couple with two cars, a one-car garage, and not a lot of money. Jane's car is four years old, John's seven. Although the cars could use frequent tune-ups, to save money each car is tuned up only once a year, usually in the fall. A fall tune-up is particularly important in the northern plains state where the Hills live, with its long and severe winters.

It is about a week before Thanksgiving. As usual, John left his car outside overnight, while Jane's was parked safely inside the garage. The weather has been unusually mild so far and John's car has been running well all summer and fall, so John has felt no urgency about tuning his car. Jane's car, however, was into the shop for a tune-up earlier this month.

On this particular morning, a problem has developed. Although the previous day was mild and sunny, a sudden cold snap set in overnight; and the temperature now is about 10 degrees above zero. John has just tried unsuccessfully to start his car. It is turning over, so the battery seems to be fine. The gas gauge reads half-full, so an empty gas tank is not the problem. Jane's car has started, and it looks as though she will have to drive John to work this morning.

What has caused John's car to fail to start?

Before discussing this case, we need to make a distinction between contributing causes and the immediate or precipitating cause of a problem. Contributing causes help to create the problem, but in and of themselves do not actually *cause* the problem. The problem is, instead, initiated by the precipitating cause.

Participants in our workshops often come up with a number of possible contributing causes for this problem (bad spark plugs, worn distributor points, and other defects that might be expected in a car that has not been tuned up in a year). But after some discussion almost everyone agrees that the *precipitating* or *most likely* cause of the problem is the cold weather, which placed too much demand on a car badly in need of a tune-up. The car had apparently started on previous mornings. Therefore, it can be assumed that if the weather had not suddenly become colder, the car probably would have started on this particular morning.

It is important to examine the mental process used to come up with the most likely cause of this problem. First, a comparison is made between John's car on the previous mornings when the problem did not exist and the current situation in which the problem does exist. Second, two crucial questions are asked: What is different between the situation in which the problem did not exist and the current situation? What has changed from then to now? The answer is that the only thing that has changed and is different is the weather, which is, therefore, the most likely cause of the problem.

The process is as simple as that. When faced with a problem in which the cause is unknown, establish a comparison and ask yourself what is different and what has changed.

Two more points about this analysis of John's car problem are worthy of mentioning:

1. ***John's car was compared with itself.*** We could have compared John's car with Jane's, but it is better to compare John's car with itself at an earlier point in time because fewer variables are involved. Although it is possible that a comparison with Jane's car might have yielded the same cause, the facts that her car was newer, had been tuned up recently, and had spent the night in the garage introduce a number of variables that would have impeded the problem analysis. As will be seen shortly, it is sometimes necessary to settle for such a comparison in working with a problem; but if possible it is always better to compare the object or situation with itself at an earlier point in time when the problem did not exist.

2. ***Although the weather has been established as the most likely cause of the car problem, it is not possible at this point to be sure that it is the actual cause.*** If the investigation were to continue, it might be discovered that some teenagers had vandalized the car overnight, disconnecting all of its wires. In every problem in which the cause is unknown, at some point the people involved in the analysis must verify the most likely cause as the actual cause. Although this may sound simple, it is surprising how often this task is skipped and actions are taken to correct a cause that has not been verified.

At the heart of causal/resource analysis lies the belief that a problem can best be understood if it is compared to another situation as much like itself as possible, but one in which the problem does not exist or is less serious. In most machine or production-line problems, this strategy is fairly obvious, although not always used. An engine that has been functioning correctly begins to misfire; a typewriter begins to skip; a bottling line begins to produce an unacceptable number of rejects. No matter how obscure the cause of any such problem may seem to be at first, a comparison of the current problem situation with the same situation at an earlier point in time when the problem did not exist or was not as serious should provide evidence that will lead to the solution of the problem. Something has to happen to change one situation into another. Change over time, therefore, becomes the clue that leads to the solution of most machine-related problems. This same strategy can be applied to some "people problems." If there has been a deterioration in performance over time, a comparison of the current situation with an earlier situation will produce evidence of the cause of the problem in much the same way as a machine problem (although often with less certainty).

In some cases the problem has always existed. Even in these cases, however, an immense amount of information can still be learned by comparing that situation to a different situation in which the problem either does not exist or does not exist to as serious a degree. If, for instance, the affirmative action program in your company not only does not seem to be working but also has never worked, you can learn a great deal about the causes of that problem by comparing your program with a more successful program in a similar company. The causes of the problem are almost certain to lie in these differences.

An emphasis on differences, however, will only help to isolate the cause of a problem; it will not isolate the means for solving that problem. Unfortunately, the similarities between a problem situation and a more desirable situation are often overlooked in a rush to solve the problem. Suppose, for instance, that your planning for the introduction of a new product does not seem to be going as well as usual. If you examine the similarities between the current problem situation and a more desirable one, it may become clear that the things that have *not* changed (your experience, for example, or your planning model) can be relied on as resources to help you work through the current difficult situation. You can turn to problem solving with a clearer understanding of your strengths.

The following sequence explains the specific steps to be taken in conducting causal/resource analysis.

STEP 1: IDENTIFY AND ANALYZE A COMPARATIVE SITUATION

To begin the process of identifying causes and resources, identify or create a situation with which the current situation can be compared. Three possible types of comparative situations are possible; they are as follows, listed in order of desirability from most to least desirable:

1. *Type A:* the situation as it currently exists compared with the same situation at some earlier point in time when the problem did not exist or was not as serious;

2. *Type B:* the situation as it currently exists compared with a similar situation in which the problem does not exist, or exists but is not as serious;[6] and

3. *Type C:* the situation as it currently exists compared with the target.

Next, using a process similar to that described in the previous chapter, identify and collect relevant information about the comparative situation in terms of *who, what, where, when, extent,* and *pattern.* The kinds of questions you should ask about the comparative situation are as follows:

- Who is involved?
- What exactly is happening?
- Where is the comparative situation?
- What objects or processes are involved?
- When is the comparative situation taking place or how recently was it taking place?
- What is the extent?
- What is the pattern?

When you complete this step in a problem-solving effort, record your answers to these questions on a form like the one presented in Figure 8.

STEP 2: COMPARE AND CONTRAST THE CURRENT AND COMPARATIVE SITUATIONS

Look for major similarities between the actual and comparative situations. What forces, motives, influences, or drives exist in both situations? Those factors that are common to both situations may be resources that will help move toward problem solution.

Then examine the actual and comparative situations for differences. Be as specific as possible in terms of *who, what, where, when, extent,* and *pattern.* When you complete this step in a problem-solving effort, record your responses on a form like the one presented in Figure 9.

---

[6]Sometimes it is possible to establish a comparative situation for either a Type A or Type B comparison in which the problem actually is worse than at present. For instance, in the previous example, you might be able to learn quite a bit from a comparison between your company's affirmative action program and one at another company that is in even worse shape. Our experience, however, indicates that in the vast majority of problems you will ever encounter, the comparative situation will be one in which the problem does not exist or is not as serious. The possibility of establishing a comparative situation in which the problem is worse should be kept in mind, though, at least as a possibility.

Who	
What	
Where	
When	
Extent	
Pattern	

**Figure 8. Form for Recording Information
About Comparative Situation**

STEP 3: IDENTIFY RESOURCES AVAILABLE TO SOLVE THE PROBLEM

Examine each similarity between the current and the comparative situation, answering these questions:

- Will this similarity help me to achieve an important goal or cluster of goals?
- Am I confident that this similarity is unlikely to change during the course of problem solving?

If the answer to these questions is "yes," then that similarity will be a significant resource in the solution of the problem.

	Information About Current Situation	**Information About Comparative Situation**
Who		
What		
Where		
When		
Extent		
Pattern		
Similarities:		
Differences:		

**Figure 9. Form for Recording Information
About Current and Comparative Situations**

STEP 4: DETERMINE THE MOST LIKELY CAUSE OF THE PROBLEM

Examine the differences between the current and the comparative situations. The most likely cause of the problem will be that potential cause that explains all of the information collected about the problem situation. When you complete this step in a problem-solving effort, record your answers to Steps 3 and 4 on a form like the one presented in Figure 10.[7]

STEP 5: DETERMINE WHETHER THE PROBLEM IS UNIQUE OR GENERIC

One of the dangers of any approach to problem solving is that it can be seen as primarily reactive. People are taught to wait for a problem to happen, then to respond. At this point in integrated problem management, however, you can begin to move out of that reactive mode by pausing a moment to consider whether the problem is unique or simply a symptom of a broader or more generic problem.

If the problem is unique, you can move on with some hope that, once it has been solved, you will not see it again. If, on the other hand, the problem is generic, you need to decide whether the symptoms are significant enough to warrant continued attention. If they are, you need to continue managing the immediate problem. Once those symptoms are under control, however, you might want to address the more generic problem by returning to the beginning of the problem-solving process. If the symptoms are not significant enough to demand immediate attention, you might want to start addressing the generic problem.

USING THE FIVE STEPS OF CAUSAL/RESOURCE ANALYSIS ON A SAMPLE PROBLEM

So that you can see how these five steps work out in actual problem solving, we have included a case study involving a problem that is far more complex than that of John's car, but that nevertheless responds to the techniques we have presented.

---

[7]For a discussion of the relationship between this part of integrated problem management and the work of Kurt Lewin, see the discussion of his "force-field analysis" in the Appendix of this book.

	Information About Current Situation	**Information About Comparative Situation**
Who		
What		
Where		
When		
Extent		
Pattern		
Similarities:		
Differences:		
Resources:		
Cause:		

Figure 10. Form for Recording Similarities,
Differences, Resources, and Cause

The Alder Lumber Company Case

☐ Alder Lumber is a small company that specializes in manufacturing expensive, natural-wood tables and chairs for a national furniture chain with an exclusive, colonial image. Because production runs at Alder are relatively short when compared with those of larger mass producers, frequent retooling and new setups are required on the three production lines that produce the majority of the company's tables and chairs. Alder's high emphasis on quality and workmanship, however, has made these changes rather easy. But on Friday, January 15th, a problem develops that is far from routine.

The Characters

Bob Keen is a planing-machine operator with nearly twenty years of experience with the company. His job is to set up and sometimes to operate the three large planing machines that begin the production-line process. A roughly shaped piece of wood is fed into one of these complicated machines, which produces a semi-sanded tabletop in about thirty seconds. Quality control is essential in Bob's job because on most runs it is three hours before the tabletops are inspected again by the fine finishers at the other end of the line. The general layout of each of the three production lines is presented in Figure 11.

Bob has an excellent record for high-quality work, although he is not well liked by most of the company's younger employees. Short-tempered and stubborn, Bob has little patience with the mistakes that those people—in his opinion—are always making.

Bert Winn is the general foreman at Alder. He is responsible for supervising all three production lines, for troubleshooting problems as they arise, and for dealing with personnel problems.

Bert has been with the company for eight years; perhaps because he tends to avoid conflict, he has established a good relationship with all of the old-timers. Bob, however, continues to regard Bert as an outsider.

Don Gilbertson is an apprentice machine operator. According to the union agreement, he is supposed to be learning his job directly from Bob. After six months at Alder Lumber, Don is beginning to complain that Bob has hardly spoken to him during all that time, much less taught him anything. Don is determined to learn the operation of the planing machines, however, even if he is not yet qualified to operate these complex machines by himself.

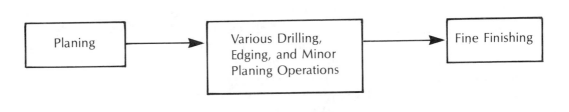

Figure 11. Layout of a Production Line at Alder Lumber Company

Steve Paulson is the production helper on Line 1. Steve has been working for Alder since his discharge from the Army three months ago. Steve's record as a computer weapons operator for the military is excellent and seemed at first to have carried over to his work at Alder. Recently, however, he has become somewhat sullen and withdrawn.

For several weeks Steve has gone out of his way to avoid contact with Bob. This is something of a problem since Steve's job is to take the tabletops out of the machine operated by Bob and stack them on a pallet before they move on to various drilling, edging, and minor planing operations. Although the job is quite routine, it is important that Steve inspect each tabletop for imperfections because it will not be handled again for three hours.

About a week ago, as he walked past Steve's car in the company parking lot, Bert noticed a new catalog from the local community college lying on the front seat.

Events of January 15th

8:00 a.m.—A new run of tabletops begins on Line 1. Bob retooled the planing machine the previous afternoon, and he supervises its operation all of this morning.

8:00 a.m.-10:00 a.m.—Production of top-quality wood tabletops continues. At 10:00 a.m. the run shifts to a lower-grade tabletop of the same dimensions.

10:00 a.m.-12 noon—Production of the lower-grade tabletops continues.

12 noon-1:00 p.m.—Lunch. All three lines are shut down for one hour. Bob rechecks his machine, makes a few minor adjustments, then moves to the planer on Line 3 for an identical setup.

1:00 p.m.-3:00 p.m.—All three lines start up at 1:00 p.m. The run on Line 1 shifts back to top-quality tabletops. Bert places Don in charge of the planing machine with strict instructions to make no adjustments without consulting Bob.

1:45 p.m.—Production of identical tabletops begins on Line 3. There seem to be no initial problems.

3:00 p.m.—Line 1 shifts once again to lower-grade tabletops.

4:00 p.m.—A few tabletops begin to show up at fine finishing on Line 1 with a one-half-inch gouge on one side.

4:55 p.m.—The number of pieces with a one-half-inch gouge has steadily increased to include almost all tabletops reaching the fine-finishing station. Bert closes down Line 1. The tabletops reaching fine finishing on Line 3 show no defects.

5:00 p.m.-5:30 p.m.—Even though quitting time is 5:00 p.m., Bert holds a quick meeting with Bob, Don, and Steve. A spot check shows that all of the tabletops coming out of the planer on Line 1 have the one-half-inch gouge, even though the roughly shaped pieces going into the machine seem to be all right. Bob is speechless with anger. Don admits to having made one minor adjustment on the planer at about 2:15 p.m., which Bob angrily points to as the cause of the problem. Steve acknowledges that he should have noticed the flaws when they started appearing but complains of a severe headache.

5:30 p.m.—Bert lets the three men leave. His boss tells him to wait until Monday morning to tackle the problem. As Bert drives home he realizes that he really has two problems: First, he has to find out what went wrong on Line 1. Second, he has to do something about Steve's negligence and the general interpersonal problems that exist.

The production-line part of the problem definitely needs causal/resource analysis. As in almost every production-line problem that we have ever seen, the target is absolutely clear: The people involved want the machine to work the way it should. Consequently, no time needs to be spent on that phase of the problem-solving process. The first thing to do, then, is to analyze the current problem situation in terms of *who*, *what*, *where*, *when*, *extent*, and *pattern*. Before proceeding, reread the case study and answer the following questions.

1. Who is involved in the problem?

2. What exactly is wrong?

3. Where is the problem taking place?

4. Where was the problem first observed?

5. Where on the objects involved is the defect occurring?

6. When did the problem begin?

7. When was the problem first observed?

8. What is the extent of the problem?

9. What is the pattern of the problem?

Compare your answers with those that follow, which are typical of the ones generated in our workshops.

1. *Who is involved in the problem?* Answer: Bob, Bert, Don, and Steve.

2. *What exactly is wrong?* Answer: One-half-inch gouges are appearing on the tabletops.

3. *Where is the problem taking place?* Answer: Apparently in the planer on Line 1.

4. *Where was the problem first observed?* Answer: At the fine-finishing station.

5. *Where on the objects involved is the defect occurring?* Answer: On one side of each tabletop involved.

6. *When did the problem begin?* Answer: Unknown at this point.

7. *When was the problem first observed?* Answer: At 4:00 p.m.

8. *What is the extent of the problem?* Answer: As of 5:00 p.m. the extent is total: "all of the tabletops coming out of the planer have the one-half-inch gouge."

9. *What is the pattern of the problem?* Answer: Steadily increasing from 4:00 p.m. to 4:55 p.m.

The next task is to choose a situation with which the current situation can be compared. Write your choice in the space that follows.

In this case there are two possible comparative situations. Line 1 can be compared with itself at some earlier point in time when the problem did not exist, or Line 1 can be compared with Line 3, which is apparently not having any problems. Which did you choose? If you chose to use Line 1 at an earlier point in time, you made the better choice; a Type A comparison will probably lead to the cause more effectively than the Type B comparison using Line 3.

Before you continue, take a few moments to do your own analysis of Line 1 *before the problem existed*. Write your responses to the following questions:

1. Who is involved?

2. What is happening?

3. Where is the problem *not* taking place?

4. When did the problem *not* exist?

Compare your answers with the ones that follow:

1. *Who is involved?* Answer: Bob, Bert, and Steve.

2. *What is happening?* Answer: Line 1 is performing up to standard.

3. *Where is the problem* not *taking place?* Answer: In the planer on Line 1.

4. *When did the problem* not *exist?* Answer: Before 1:00 p.m.

Were you able to figure out the response to the last question? The case study says that it takes three hours for the tabletops to move from the planer to fine finishing. The defective tabletops were first observed at fine finishing at 4:00 p.m., which means that the problem must have begun at 1:00 p.m. If you wish, you can now take that new information and plug it into the analysis of the current situation in response to the question "When did the problem first begin?" In this case the "extent" and "pattern" questions are irrelevant, so they do not appear.

The similarities between the two situations are Bert, Steve, Bob, the machinery, and the raw materials. These similarities confirm Bert's belief that he can rely on Bob's experience, the essential quality of the machines, and the raw materials as resources in solving the production-line part of the problem. The differences involve Don, Bob, and two minor adjustments. These differences identify the only three changes that have taken place between the time when things were going well and when the current problem began. Bob has grabbed at the most obvious change, the minor adjustment that Don made in the planer at 2:15 p.m. This, however, cannot be the cause of the problem because it does not explain all of the facts. It takes three hours for the tabletops to move from the planer to fine finishing; and any defects caused by Don's adjustment would not show up until 5:15 p.m., well after the actual problem developed. The most likely cause of the problem, therefore, must be one of the few "minor adjustments" that Bob made during lunch. This analysis is summarized in Figure 12.

Later Bert verified that one of Bob's adjustments had, in fact, caused the production-line part of the problem; Bob had inadvertently loosened an important guide that allowed a slight slip in the path of the tabletops. As the afternoon wore on, that guide became looser and looser, accounting for the increased number of gouges by the end of the afternoon.

Bert used part of his weekend to go through a complete causal/resource analysis of the production-line part of the problem. With the "people" part of the problem, however, he took a few shortcuts and used only those parts of the process that were relevant. (This is fairly typical of the way in which most people use integrated problem management; as we have said several times, use only those parts of the process that you need, solve the problem, and return to what you were doing before the problem required your attention.) The target was fairly clear, if not quite as obvious as with

	Information About Current Situation	Information About Comparative Situation
Who	Bob, Bert, Don, and Steve	Bob, Bert, and Steve
What	½" gouge on tabletops	Line 1 performing up to standard
Where	Apparently taking place in the planer; first observed at fine finishing	In the planer on Line 1
When	4:00 p.m. (first observed)	Before 1:00 p.m.
Extent	Total	
Pattern	Steadily increasing	

Similarities: Bert, Bob, and Steve
The machinery
The raw materials

Differences: Don and Bob
The two minor adjustments

Resources: Bob's experience
The quality of the machinery
The raw materials

Cause: The adjustment made at lunchtime

**Figure 12. Analysis of Production-Line Problem
at Alder Lumber Company**

the production-line part of the problem: Bert wanted to see to it that Steve was working up to his potential; he wanted Bob to become more cooperative and helpful in his relationships with Don, Steve, and himself; and he wanted to make sure that Don was trained.

Bert first turned his attention to Steve. He saw immediately that the situation called for a Type A comparison, in which he could compare Steve's currently poor performance first with his more motivated performance as a weapons operator in the Army and second with his performance in his first few weeks at Alder. The answer to the questions "What is different?" and "What has changed?" seemed obvious: In the Army Steve had a demanding, technical job with considerable individual responsibility. His positive work habits had carried over at first to Alder but gradually deteriorated in the face of the relatively boring, repetitive work of a production helper. Bert had not yet come up with a solution to the problem with Steve, but he had identified the most likely cause of Steve's poor performance. He made a mental note to have a talk with Steve to check this out.

Bob presented Bert with a more difficult problem. This seemed to involve a Type C comparison, in which Bob's presently poor attitude would have to be contrasted to the target identified earlier. The answer to the key question "What would have to change to make the current situation more like the desired situation?" was obviously Bob's attitude or behavior. Bert could, of course, attempt to analyze the causes of Bob's generally negative attitude, but that seemed like a job for a psychoanalyst, not a foreman. Bert was not so unrealistic as to expect Bob to become the "ideal employee," but he did feel that he needed some ideas about what he might do to help Bob start working more cooperatively with others. He needed some creative proposals for action.

Finally, Bert examined all of the separate problems he had identified to determine which ones were unique and which were generic. The mistake that Bob made in adjusting the machine on Line 1 was certainly unique; despite all of his difficulties with Bob, Bert had absolute confidence in Bob's technical abilities. He also felt that the interpersonal problems he was having with both Bob and Steve were one-time-only concerns and that both men were assets to the company. Bert was convinced that it was appropriate to proceed in working toward solutions of these unique problems.

Bert did feel, however, that he was also facing two generic problems. The first was the three-hour gap between quality-control inspections on all three production lines. This was not the first time that he had experienced this kind of delay in noticing production-line problems. The second had to do with the difficulty of implementing certain aspects of the union contract, such as the union stipulation that Don learn his job directly from Bob; this kind of problem also had occurred before. Bert decided that once he had resolved the more immediate, unique problems with Bob and Steve he would talk with his supervisor about ways to address these two generic problems.

Notice the flexible way in which Bert used the process of causal/resource analysis. The production-line part of the problem obviously required a detailed use of this process; but when Bert approached his problem with Steve, he did not bother with the *who, what, where, when, extent,* and *pattern* questions. Instead, he went right to the heart of the matter by asking "What has changed from the time when Steve was performing well to now?" Finally, Bert had the sense not even to try to use causal/resource analysis in solving his problem with Bob. Although Bob might at one time have been a more cooperative employee, that time would have been so long ago that a comparison between then and now would have been useless. Bert knew that he needed some new ideas about what to do with Bob. How he came up with those ideas is the subject of the next chapter.

9

Generating Proposals

By this time you may have a very clear idea of what needs to be done to solve some of the problems we have presented so far: John needs to have his car tuned up; Larry needs to return to his department full-time to help Frank with the Christmas rush. But what about the problem faced by Bert at Alder Lumber Company? The adjustment that Bob made obviously needs to be corrected, but what is to be done about Steve's poor performance and Bob's interpersonal difficulties? At this point Bert needs to come up with some good proposals that may solve the different aspects of the problem.

Unfortunately, people face several major barriers when they attempt to come up with creative ideas or proposals for solving problems:

1. **The human mind has been programed to recognize patterns and to behave accordingly.** Crossing a street, driving a car, and carrying on a social conversation are all patterned behaviors. Much of problem solving is also patterned. People encounter problems similar to ones that they have confronted before, and they go about solving the new problems in a similar manner. Unfortunately, this patterned approach may not be as successful in solving a new problem. Nor will it provide new insights on old ones.

2. **People have been trained to reject new ideas.** Regardless of how much education they have had, schooling teaches them to respond critically to ideas that are new or different, to look immediately for reasons that proposals will not work. Do the following comments sound familiar?

- "It isn't in the budget."
- "It won't work in our company."
- "We tried that before."
- "It's too radical."
- "We don't have the time."
- "We're too small (big) for something like that."
- "We've never done it before."
- "You can't teach an old dog new tricks."
- "Let's put it on the back burner for now."
- "Let's form a committee to study it."
- "No one else has ever tried it."
- "It's against company policy."

71

These "killer phrases" have traditionally been used to stop progress. When people get together to tackle a problem, standard operating procedure seems to be to criticize one another's ideas.

3. **People place a premium on being "right."** From earliest childhood they are taught not to make mistakes. It is almost as if the "killer phrases" are internalized to the point that people are critical of their own ideas, even when they work alone. More than anything else, this fear of making a mistake, of appearing foolish or stupid even to oneself, limits creativity.

4. **The harder people try to be creative at problem solving, the less likely it is that they will come up with good ideas.** Creative problem solving is primarily a right-brain activity. The harder people try to shift from the rational and logical left brain to the creative and playful right, the less success they have; that shift almost always takes place when people are *not* trying.

Therefore, to generate creative ideas that can be considered as proposals for solving a problem, you must learn to turn off your internal censor, that little voice inside you that says "that won't work," "that's a dumb idea," "that's crazy." You must learn that it is all right to be wrong, to make mistakes. You also must find ways of breaking the patterns of your usual thinking. When you work with a group, you and the other members must withhold criticism and evaluation, at least for a while. Finally, and paradoxically, you must learn not to try too hard to be creative.

STEP 1: GENERATE DIVERGENT PROPOSALS FOR SOLVING THE PROBLEM

"Creativity" is not easily defined; people often disagree about its meaning. What one person considers creative might appear strange, crazy, or perhaps just obvious to others.

Nevertheless, there are still a few things that can be said in general about creativity. Three conditions tend to generate it:

1. **Regressing or moving backward to some more elementary, primitive, or childlike mode of thinking.** People are often more creative, for instance, when they can create an image of a problem rather than think about it. The best ideas often come not when people are fully awake, but when they are falling asleep, waking up, or dreaming. When working on his highly creative and complex theory of relativity, Albert Einstein often examined various ideas on the basis of visual symmetry rather than logic. Reportedly he experienced some ideas as actually "tasting good" to him. To be creative, people must detach themselves from their usual, logical, language-based mode of problem solving.

2. **Getting away from the problem for a while.** Creative solutions to complex problems often do not emerge when the problem is first confronted but instead after a period of *incubation*. In some manner a corner of the mind keeps working on the problem while one is attending to other matters. A creative proposal often comes to mind fully developed after a period of days or even weeks—often to the surprise of the person who comes up with the idea. By setting problems aside for a while, people create the possibility that these problems will be treated in a more creative, regressive manner than if they receive full and direct attention.

3. *Creating a "safe" environment in which new and tentative ideas can be expressed without being evaluated.* Researchers on creativity have found that a group of people working in such an environment can generate more creative ideas than in an environment characterized by evaluation. The key to this creativity is "synergy," a cooperative interaction between people and ideas that produces something that is greater than the sum of its parts.

The major task involved in creative problem solving is to create a situation in which these three conditions can exist. Although a wide range of approaches can be taken to this task, our research has brought us to the conclusion that there are basically three ways of generating creative ideas as proposals for solving problems: People can release their energy to address the problem; they can change the shape or form of the problem; or they can create an analogy related to the problem.

Releasing Energy to Address the Problem

Divergent thinking is creative, exciting, spontaneous, unpredictable, and above all energetic. Sometimes the energy for creativity is clearly present and easily available as an individual or a group attacks a problem. At such times the task may be simply to keep the creative process flowing and to record the results of that effort. Unfortunately, these situations are relatively rare. In most cases people must release the energy necessary to generate proposals. Old barriers need to be broken; detours around old ways of thinking need to be found; and creativity needs to be set free.

Releasing energy in this way is a matter of some skill. The following discussion outlines three ways of doing this. Each is less structured that the previous one, but all three require careful selection and planning. Properly used, however, each has been found effective in supplying the energy required to create a variety of possible solutions.

All three of these strategies can be used for individual as well as group problem solving; we describe them first as group activities and then later explain how to alter them for individual use. All three require careful consideration of the problem statement being addressed. In general, the more specific the problem statement is, the more focused will be the proposals that are generated. A problem statement such as "How can we increase our sales?" will elicit more diverse proposals than will the statement "How can we increase our sales to female teen-agers on Saturdays?" When taking on a problem for the first time, however, a broad problem statement may be appropriate. In these cases follow-up sessions may be needed as different aspects of the problem become more focused.

1. *Nominal group technique (Delbecq & Van de Ven, 1971).* This technique is a highly structured process for generating possible solutions to a problem statement. Independently, and without discussion, group members write lists of alternative solutions to the problem at hand. At least fifteen minutes should be allowed for this activity. The members are instructed to remain quiet once they have completed their own lists, both to give them an opportunity to reflect on what they have written and to allow those who have not finished to complete their work more easily.

Once the initial time period has elapsed and without any preliminary discussion, one of the members reads aloud the first item on his or her list, which is then recorded in full view of all members. The next member reads his or her first item, which is also recorded. This process continues, with each member reading only one item at a time, until all ideas have been listed. Overlap of ideas should not be of concern at this point. As new ideas occur to people, they are to be written as additions to the members' original lists and then read aloud when these members take their turns.

A period of approximately fifteen to twenty minutes is then allowed for discussion of individual items. This discussion, which is intended only to provide clarification and understanding of each item, should be as nonevaluative as possible. Duplicates may be eliminated at this point, and new ideas that occur to people during the discussion are recorded on the master list.

The nominal group technique concludes with another period of silence, during which the members are asked to sit quietly and reflect on the process they have just completed. Any new ideas that come to them during this reflection are to be silently noted and then, at the end of this final period, recorded on the master list.

2. **Divergent Delphi method.** This technique has been derived from the conventional Delphi method (Dalkey & Helmer, 1963), which seeks convergence or consensus from the members of a group on a specific issue or problem. The *divergent* Delphi method, by contrast, encourages—and even forces—group members to generate responses that lie outside the mid-range. These responses, which are often irrelevant, humorous, intriguing, or just "off the wall," can be a source of genuinely creative proposals.

Using the divergent Delphi method is quite simple. Each member, in turn, makes a proposal for the solution of the problem confronting the group. Once a proposal has been made, it can no longer be offered as a suggestion by any other group member. A specific number of rounds (three or four for a large group, ten or more for a small group) are specified. Passing is not allowed.

Usually the opening rounds go rather quickly as obvious suggestions are offered. The process becomes much more interesting in the following rounds, however, as new and more creative ideas are presented. Evaluation occurs only if an idea is unacceptably close to one that has been offered previously, although building on previous suggestions is encouraged. All ideas are recorded for later discussion.

The participants in this process should be encouraged to use humor and analogy. Each member is required to present an idea when his or her turn comes, even if no solutions come readily to mind. When given the permission to pull ideas out of "left field" or make really "bad" suggestions, people often generate what ultimately may become their most creative and valuable suggestions.

3. **Brainstorming.** This term is often used to label almost any loosely structured group discussion; brainstorming is, in fact, a very specific technique that demands a certain amount of organization. Brainstorming can be used by a group to generate a large number of proposals in a short period of time. Five stages are involved:

- *Stage 1: Set a time limit for the brainstorm.* A period of three to five minutes is usually sufficient; when necessary, the session can be started again after a review of the ideas generated during the first period.
- *Stage 2: Review the rules of brainstorming.* The group members are to offer any and all ideas that come to mind during the brainstorming period. Each idea is to be recorded but not evaluated. Any critical comments or words of praise for an idea are to be avoided or cut off. The members are encouraged to build on one another's ideas, to use humor, to feel free to be irrelevant, and to articulate everything that comes to mind. They are to state their ideas without explaining or enlarging on them or attempting to justify them; these more conceptual activities come after the brainstorming period has been concluded.

- *Stage 3: Practice (optional).* If a group has never conducted a brainstorm, it may wish to "warm up" by either performing a brief brainstorm on some irrelevant topic (for example, "How might the standard credit card be redesigned to prevent theft?") or by requesting each member of the group to verbalize one "bad," irrelevant, or mundane idea about the problem before starting the brainstorm.
- *Stage 4: Select one or more members of the group as recorders whose job is to write down all of the ideas generated.* At least one recorder should be appointed for every five members. Because many people find inspiration in the previously recorded ideas of others, all ideas should be recorded in full view of all members. The recorders should freely record their own ideas, stating them aloud while writing them down so that the other members can hear these ideas.
- *Stage 5: Conduct the brainstorm.* Typically a group generates at least twenty ideas per minute. Most brainstorms become particularly valuable during the second or third minutes after standard ideas have been expressed and the group members begin exploring new areas. The brainstorm should always be brought to a close when the time limit is reached.

As we mentioned previously, it is also possible to use any of these three strategies when you are working on a problem individually rather than in a group setting. You can perform your own version of the divergent Delphi method by making a list of possible solutions, none of which repeats any of the earlier ones, or by requiring yourself to add a new and different item to the list every minute for a half-hour.

You can also use the nominal group technique or brainstorming on your own. In a quiet place free of interruptions, simply sit for a while and let your mind wander as you think about the problem. Then, for a period of five minutes, focus your energy by writing down every possible solution that comes to your mind. Do not try to be "right" or "brilliant" or even "creative"; just list all of the ideas that you can. Your list should be as long and full as possible; quantity, not quality, is the objective. After this five-minute period, again sit quietly and reflect on what you have done, adding any final ideas that come to mind.

When working alone you might want to set the problem aside for a day or two after your initial session to allow your unconscious to work on the problem. Additional insights and potential solutions often present themselves either during this period or during a second round of work.

Although the nominal group technique and the divergent Delphi method may not have been familiar to you, probably you have had some contact with brainstorming and thus have some idea of what it can produce: a large number of ideas, some obvious, some crazy or just plain silly, and some genuinely creative. Our experience, however, is that although people are willing to use all three of these strategies in workshops, they hesitate to try them in "real-world" settings. Do not let this happen to you; try using these strategies when appropriate in your next meeting or when attempting to solve your next real problem. We are confident that they will work for you.

Changing the Shape or Form of the Problem

The second way to generate creative ideas involves changing the shape or form of the problem. Many people who are considered by others to be creative seem to use this process naturally. By in some way transforming the problem into something else for a while, they are able to come back to the original problem with some genuinely new ideas. The famous nine-dot puzzle (see Figure 13) provides an example of changing the shape of the problem. The task presented by the puzzle is to connect the nine dots by drawing only four straight-line segments, never lifting the pencil from the paper until the task has been completed. The solution, as shown in Figure 14, requires that one go outside the square implied by the nine dots.

Similarly, by changing the shape of a problem, you force yourself outside the implied framework of the original problem. In thinking about that reshaped problem, you may actually come up with some new ideas that will be useful in solving the real problem.

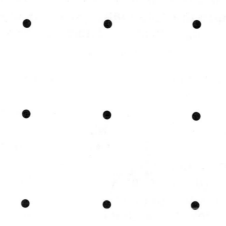

Figure 13. Nine-Dot Puzzle

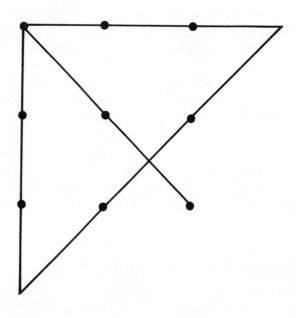

Figure 14. Solution to Nine-Dot Puzzle

Alex Osborn (1979), the creator of brainstorming, offers the following list of questions to help in reshaping a problem:[8]

1. ***Put to other uses?*** New ways to use as is? Other ideas if modified?

2. ***Adapt?*** What else is like this? What other idea does this suggest? Does past offer a parallel? What could I copy? Whom could I emulate?

3. ***Modify?*** New twist? Change meaning, color, motion, sound, odor, form, shape? Other changes?

4. ***Magnify?*** What to add? More time? Greater frequency? Stronger? Higher? Longer? Thicker? Extra value? Plus ingredient? Duplicate? Multiply? Exaggerate?

5. ***Minify?*** What to subtract? Smaller? Condensed? Miniature? Lower? Shorter? Lighter? Omit? Streamline? Split up? Understate?

6. ***Substitute?*** Who else instead? What else instead? Other ingredient? Other material? Other process? Other power? Other place? Other approach? Other tone of voice?

7. ***Rearrange?*** Interchange components? Other pattern? Other layout? Other sequence? Transpose cause and effect? Change pace? Change schedule?

8. ***Reverse?*** Transpose positive and negative? How about opposites? Turn it backward? Turn it upside down? Reverse roles? Change shoes? Turn tables? Turn other cheek?

9. ***Combine?*** How about a blend, an alloy, an assortment, an ensemble? Combine units? Combine purposes? Combine appeals? Combine ideas?

The following are some examples of ways to reshape the problems we have presented so far in examples and case studies:

- Larry might discover some new approaches to solving the problem with Frank Foster if he were to imagine that he is in Frank's place and Frank is in his, that Frank's difficulties involve drugs and alcohol instead of customer complaints and sick days, that his new boss Nancy does not need any help from him in becoming settled in her job, or that Nancy needs him full-time for the next six months.

- The president of King Printing Corporation might attack his excess-paperwork problem by imagining what he would do if the size of his company doubled in two months; if the company were half of its present size but with paperwork at its current level; or if Joe, the vice president for whom there is no replacement, suddenly died.

- Bert at Alder Lumber Company might imagine that Steve is the boss's son or a brilliant but unemployed Ph.D. candidate. He might try to figure out what he would do if Bob and Don or Bob and Steve were to switch jobs. He might even go so far as to imagine himself as president of Alder, with Bob, Don, and Steve as his three vice presidents.

Once the problem has been reshaped, it can be attacked directly or with any of the strategies for releasing energy that have been discussed previously.

---

[8]Alex F. Osborn, excerpted from APPLIED IMAGINATION 3rd Edition. Copyright © 1963 Charles Scribner's Sons. Reprinted with the permission of Charles Scribner's Sons, a division of Macmillan, Inc.

Changing the form of a problem does not always help, of course. But even if no new ideas emerge from dealing with the reshaped problem, our experience is that people return to their real problems refreshed and sometimes even with a sense of relief that the real circumstances are not as bad as the imagined ones. Also, you should remember that the purpose of creative problem solving is not to come up with a completely worked-out solution in a brilliant flash of insight. It is, instead, to open up the problem a bit so that you can continue working with it by looking at it from a new angle.

Ultimately, reshaping the problem is what actually did help Bert to achieve solutions at Alder Lumber Company. The thought of Steve as a Ph.D. candidate helped Bert to focus on the difference between Steve's Army background and his current job. Then Bert remembered that he had seen a college catalog in Steve's car and realized that a future on a production line did not make any sense for Steve. After talking with Bert, Steve agreed and left Alder to attend the local community college; however, he continued to work at Alder during summers and vacations (enthusiastically, as a welcome break from his books). The last news we heard was that Steve was interviewing for entry-level management positions and that one of the companies he was looking at was Alder.

Creating an Analogy Related to the Problem

The third way to generate creative ideas involves thinking in terms of analogies. An analogy establishes a comparison between two events, people, objects, or activities that may or may not be very much alike. Some analogies are quite simple, such as thinking of the heart as a pump or food as fuel for the body. Others may be more unusual, such as those in the titles of Hemingway's "Hills Like White Elephants" and F. Scott Fitzgerald's *Tender Is the Night.*

To use analogies for the purpose of problem solving, identify some other problem, experience, or field of activity that in some way is like the problem you are addressing. There are two ways of doing this:

1. ***Simply examine the problem situation for obvious analogies.*** For example, Bert at Alder Lumber Company might have thought of himself as the father of three uncooperative children, or he might have explored the ways in which Bob's relationship with Don was like a difficult father-son relationship.

2. ***Identify three or four images or areas of activity that have absolutely nothing to do with the problem, and then force an analogy between each of those images and the problem situation.*** In using this approach with the problems at Alder, one might think of random images like these: a rock-music group, the Oregon coast, a personal computer, and summertime. Then an analogy is forced between each of these images and Bert's problems with Bob, Steve, and Don:

- *A rock-music group.* Bert, Bob, Steve, and Don sound like rock-group members who cannot get along with one another. Who would be the lead singer in that group? If you were the business manager of that group, what would you do to solve the members' problems?

- *The Oregon coast.* In spite of its beauty, this coast is a relatively hostile place, particularly in the winter; yet thousands of people have learned to live with that hostility and even to love it. Are there any ways in which Bert can learn to live with his problems and Bob's hostility toward his fellow workers?

- *A personal computer.* Personal computers meet the needs of individuals; thus, most people who buy such computers shop around quite a bit to find ones that meet their unique needs. What are the unique needs of each of the four people in this situation? Is there any way for each of them to select the solution that fits those needs, just as a computer buyer selects the personal computer that is best for him or her?
- *Summertime.* Summertime is vacation time. When Bob goes on his vacation, who takes over? Since Bob has been with the company for so many years, he must have fairly substantial vacation time; and certainly Alder does not shut down its three production lines to accommodate Bert's vacation. Perhaps the individual who takes his place during his vacation could be brought into this situation.

Of course, all of these analogies do not necessarily help; but they all serve to increase perspective on the problem. In this case one analogy actually did help. Bert became interested in looking at Bob and Don's relationship as that existing between a father and son who are having difficulties. Bert had had some problems with his own son several years earlier and had found the intervention of a third party helpful. The idea of third-party intervention made Bert think of the shop steward, a highly respected senior employee who had been with the company even longer than Bob. Bert talked with the shop steward about the union's commitment to train apprentices like Don and about the current problems between Bob and Don. The shop steward, in turn, talked with Bob about his responsibility as a member of the union to train Don. Because of his respect for the steward and his life-long involvement in the union, Bob began training Don. Bob did not become an "ideal" employee, but Bert had never hoped for that. A simple analogy involving thinking of Bob and Don as father and son led fairly directly to the solution of at least that part of Bert's problem.

STEP 2: GENERATE CONVERGENT PROPOSALS TO SOLVE THE PROBLEM

Once you have generated creative ideas, it is time to bring your critical abilities into action in testing your ideas or proposals against reality. The objective of this step is to produce a more limited list of possible actions; final proposal selection is a separate process that is described in the next chapter. Consequently, if at this stage you are at all in doubt about the potential value of an idea, retain it for further consideration.

The worst thing you can do at this point in the problem-solving process is to write off the previous creative activity as fun but useless. Instead, use your critical abilities as an ally, not an enemy, of your creative ideas.

Begin by reviewing the ideas that have been generated in Step 1. Be sure you understand their implications and possible insights. Any ideas that are obviously unrelated to the problem at hand should be eliminated from further consideration.

The strengths and weaknesses of each remaining idea should then be assessed in light of the causes of the problem and the resources available for its solution. Ask yourself questions such as these: Does the idea attack the cause of the problem? Does it make use of important available resources? If an idea does not clearly address the cause of the problem or if its implementation would require extensive resources that are not currently available, eliminate it.

Next examine the remaining ideas for their positive points. Although sometimes this analysis may seem difficult, emphasizing the positive is another way of building on the ideas you have generated instead of destroying them through premature, negative evaluation.

Once the positive aspects have been identified, explore the negative aspects of each idea by asking yourself these questions:

- Why is it that this idea is not any better than it is?

- What are my primary concerns about it?

- How could it be improved?

Throughout this analysis keep in mind the "killer phrases" identified at the beginning of this chapter. Be sure that your evaluations are based on sound logic and reasoning and are not just negative responses to new ideas.

After the remaining ideas have been reviewed and judged, some may need to be dropped or significantly modified. Others can be combined. The final list of alternative ideas or proposals should be as short as possible; however, you should avoid combining too many ideas into a single, overly complex proposal. Finally, review each of the resulting proposals by referring to the *who, what, where, when, extent,* and *pattern* categories and asking these questions:

- Who will do the work involved, and who will be affected by this proposal? What are the responses or reactions of those affected likely to be?

- What will this proposal accomplish, and what will be left to do after the proposal has been implemented?

- Where will this proposal be implemented, and where are difficulties in implementation likely to arise?

- When will this proposal be implemented, and when are difficulties in implementation likely to occur?

- Will this proposal completely or only partially reduce the extent of the problem or change the pattern of the problem?

By this time you will have reduced your choices to a manageable few. If one alternative clearly leaps out, you may want to proceed to planning and implementation. However, if you are still uncertain about which proposal to choose as the solution, the suggestions on proposal selection in the next chapter should be helpful.

REFERENCES

Dalkey, N.C., & Helmer, O. (1963, April). An experimental application of the Delphi method to the use of experts. *Management Science*, p. 102.

Delbecq, A., & Van de Ven, A. (1971). A group process model for problem identification and program planning. *Journal of Applied Behavioral Science, 7,* 466-491.

Osborn, A. (1979). *Applied imagination* (3rd ed.). New York: Charles Scribner's.

10

Selecting the Best Proposals

Generating proposals can be exciting and absorbing. Divergent thinking can lead to the creation of a variety of new and fascinating possibilities, while convergent thinking can produce ingenious and logically defensible solutions. Sometimes this process results in the creation or identification of a single apparent solution, and those involved in problem solving can move directly into planning and implementation. In other cases, however, a single solution is not yet apparent. Instead, those involved may be faced with several alternatives, all of which seem responsive to the problem.

Proposals must be judged on the basis of their apparent validity and in light of the goals established for the solution of the problem. In selecting one or more proposals for implementation, you must return to the beginning of the problem-solving sequence and ask if the solution you are considering is likely to accomplish your most important goals, those most centrally located on your target. The four steps outlined in this chapter can assist you in this process.

STEP 1: EVALUATE PROPOSALS

Each alternative proposal must meet the following four criteria:

1. **Appropriateness.** Does the proposal respond to the cause of the problem? You should be able to provide a detailed scenario that describes how the proposal will transform the present situation into the target state.

2. **Attainability.** Can the proposal be successfully implemented, given your analysis of current or anticipated resources? You should be able to identify which current resources will be used to implement the proposal and where any additional resources that are needed will come from.

3. **Attractiveness.** Will the people involved in the implementation of the proposal find it attractive? You should be able to show how this particular proposal is more relevant and feasible than the others, how those involved will be able to understand and support the proposal, and how they will feel at least some degree of ownership of it.

4. **Adaptability.** Can the proposal be modified easily if conditions change or if new information is generated? You should be able to show how the solution can be divided into parts so that some parts can be implemented as originally planned and others can be modified or discarded.

On the basis of this analysis, the most appropriate solution is selected for implementation. This process can be used effectively in addressing the situation at King Printing Corporation, for example. You will recall that the president of that company was actually faced with several problems at once. The most obvious problem was the increasing amount of administrative paperwork that Joe, the vice president, was not delegating and for which he had not been hired. In addition, there was the problem of Joe's retirement in the next few years; for some reason the president was not satisfied with any of the other four managers as replacements for Joe. Also, the president's relationship with Joe was businesslike, not personal or especially comfortable. Finally, there was the amount of time that the president was spending away from the company, both developing new clients and establishing guidelines for vocational education.

The president's first proposal was to create the position of administrative manager; the person filling this position would handle the administrative-paperwork problem and learn the business so that he or she could take over when Joe retires. However, as you probably remember, it turned out that several goals would not be met by this proposal. Those goals, as listed in Chapter 7 according to priority, were as follows:

1. Handle the administrative-paperwork problem.
2. Establish better relations between Joe and the president.
3. Decide what to do when Joe retires.
4. Resolve the president's reservations about the other four managers.
5. Keep the president uninvolved in day-to-day operations.
6. Allow the president to continue developing new clients in the region.
7. Allow the president to continue working on establishing vocational-education guidelines.

When the goals were placed on a target, it became apparent that Goals 2, 3, and 4, which have to do with the interpersonal problems at the company, cluster together, are somewhat separate from Goal 1, and are in opposition to the last three goals. Having stressed the danger of accepting the first proposed solution to a problem, in this case the president's proposal to create a new managerial position, we left King Printing Corporation at this point.

When we use this case study in our workshops, the participants usually generate a list of creative proposals that looks something like this:

- Sell the company to Joe and the other four managers.
- Conduct a research study on the exact nature of the administrative paperwork.
- Hire an administrative assistant for Joe to handle the paperwork.
- Establish a management-development program for the president, Joe, and the other four managers.
- Fire Joe and force one of the other managers into his position.
- Fire Joe and force the president into his position.
- Fire the president.
- Arrange early retirement for Joe.
- Send Joe to the moon.
- Send the president to the moon.

- Take all of the managers, including Joe and the president, on a retreat somewhere with a consultant to help them work out their problems.
- Talk with Joe about when he is going to retire.
- Go ahead with the idea of a new administrative manager.
- Get the president more involved in the details of daily operation.
- Computerize the paperwork.
- Conduct a series of team-building workshops for the president, Joe, and the other four managers.
- Persuade the president to take early retirement.
- Reduce the size and scope of the company's operations to reduce the amount of paperwork.
- Have the president stop working on establishing vocational-education guidelines.
- Hire an assistant to the sales manager to help develop new business.
- Close the company.
- Merge the company into another, larger corporation.
- Find out what is wrong with the other four managers as replacements for Joe.

When we ask the participants to examine such a list rationally, most agree that certain items (like sending Joe or the president to the moon or firing either of them) can be eliminated from further consideration. The remaining items seem to cluster into one of five areas:

1. Reduce or eliminate the problem by reducing, eliminating, or substantially changing the nature of the company;
2. Create one or more new positions or methods to handle the problem;
3. Involve the president more in the operation of the company;
4. Help the current managers to do a better job; and
5. Collect more information.

After further discussion the first cluster is usually eliminated; although the president does not want to be involved in the daily operations, there is no indication that he wants to get rid of the company entirely. Then the remaining four clusters are generally combined into two alternative proposals:

1. **Alternative 1.** Collect more information about the current situation, particularly about the nature of the administrative-paperwork problem, and, on the basis of that information, create one or more new positions or employ appropriate new technologies or methods to solve the problem.

2. **Alternative 2.** Involve the president, Joe, and the other four managers in solving the problem through some kind of management-development or training program. This would require the involvement of the president for at least the time it would take to solve the problem.

When these two alternative proposals are evaluated in terms of whether they meet the four criteria that we discussed previously—appropriateness, attainability, attractiveness, and adaptability—the analysis usually resembles the following:

1. ***Is the proposal appropriate? Does it respond to the cause of the problem?***
Answer: Alternative 1 addresses only the paperwork problem. Alternative 2 at least
has the potential of dealing with the problems of the paperwork, Joe's retirement, the
qualifications of the other four managers, and the president's role in the company.
Therefore, on the basis of this criterion, Alternative 2 is preferable.

2. ***Is the proposal attainable? Can it be successfully implemented given
current or anticipated resources?*** Answer: Both proposals would require the ex-
penditure of some resources, either to collect additional information or to involve the
president, Joe, and the other four managers in the solution process. Thus, on the basis
of this criterion, the two alternatives are about equal.

3. ***Is the proposal attractive? Will the people involved understand and support it?*** Answer: Both proposals are reasonably attractive. Alternative 1 is rational,
logical, and certainly would have the support of the president because it would keep
him uninvolved in the day-to-day affairs of the company. On the other hand, Alternative
2 may well be more attractive to Joe and the other managers because it would involve
them directly in the problem-solving process. If the president were willing to become
more involved in the company for the time needed to solve the problem, Alternative
2 would be more attractive.

4. ***Is the proposal adaptable? Can it be modified if conditions change?***
Answer: Both proposals seem adaptable. Alternative 1 could be changed as additional
information is collected, and Alternative 2 would be implemented in a series of steps
over time and also could be changed as new information came to light. On the basis
of this criterion, the two alternatives are about equal.

Although the discussions that take place in the different workshops that we conduct
do not always follow this exact pattern, almost everyone eventually comes to agree that
Alternative 2 is the more desirable proposal because it is more *appropriate* and *attractive* than Alternative 1, while at the same time at least as *attainable* and *adaptable*.

Problem solving is an art, not a science; subtle judgment calls are often necessary
to determine whether one proposal is more appropriate, attainable, attractive, or adaptable than the others. In the vast majority of problems you will encounter in which
a choice must be made among competing proposals, using these four criteria will make
the best alternative apparent. However, at times you may evaluate your proposals in
terms of the four criteria and still feel unable to choose. You may feel that you do not
have enough information about how a particular proposal will work, or you may not
be able to make clear distinctions among several alternatives. In these cases you can
take one of two steps: (1) conduct a pilot test or (2) quantify the alternatives. These
two optional steps are discussed in the paragraphs that follow.

STEP 2: CONDUCT A PILOT TEST (OPTIONAL)

There are two primary reasons for conducting a pilot test. First, you may still have
some unanswered questions regarding the problem's cause, available resources, or ac-
ceptability. Just as an aviation engineer must rely on a wind-tunnel test to provide
answers to certain complex questions about design, you might have to use a pilot test

to provide answers to lingering questions about specific proposals for solving a problem. Second, a pilot test provides a safe environment in which people who are to help implement a proposal can learn new skills, gain necessary knowledge, and acquire additional experience before engaging in the full-scale implementation of that proposal as the solution to the problem. Much as a novice pilot practices in the safe but realistic cockpit of a simulated aircraft, so can those involved in a pilot test work in a setting in which mistakes can be made, new skills and knowledge can be acquired, and alternatives can be tried at minimal cost.

If a pilot test is being initiated to answer certain lingering questions, those questions, of course, should be clarified before the pilot test is designed. Among the questions that a pilot test can most successfully address are the following:

- Is the problem at least partially resolved by the tested proposal?
- Given the results of the pilot test, was the original analysis of the problem correct?
- Was the original assessment of available resources correct?
- Are the people involved with the implementation of the pilot test convinced about the probable effectiveness of the proposal?
- Do the people involved have the necessary skills to implement this proposal? What additional skills, if any, do they need?

A pilot test should not be initiated without a clear understanding of which of these questions are to be answered.

Several considerations should be kept in mind when planning a pilot test:

1. **Remember that the test is not the "real thing."** It may be that you do not need to test all components of the proposal, but only those about which uncertainty exists. A pilot test need not replicate all aspects of the problem. It is not a "dry run" of the proposed solution, except in those rare cases in which the overall proposal must be evaluated through a full-scale dress rehearsal.

2. **Do not expect complete success.** You should be able to get a taste of the solution—enough to modify it, if necessary, and enough for other people to understand what it is about and how it will work. If too much time and too many resources are expended on the pilot test, the energy that remains afterward may not be enough for a full-scale implementation.

3. **Make sure that the pilot test is carefully monitored and its results recorded.** Just as a wind-tunnel test would be useless without accurate data about the results, a pilot test would be of little value without a clear record of what happened. Depending on the nature of the pilot test, this can be accomplished through means such as first-hand observation and record keeping, videotape, narratives, performance charts, or questionnaires.

Once the pilot test has been concluded or at one or more points during the test, the information that is gathered should be examined and used, when appropriate, to modify the proposal, to seek additional support, to correct the causal/resource analysis, or to explore an alternative proposal. When these assessments have been made and one or more pilot tests have been conducted, you should be ready to formulate and implement one or more full-scale solutions to the problem.

STEP 3: QUANTIFY THE ALTERNATIVES (OPTIONAL)

Occasionally when you are unable to choose among alternative proposals, a pilot test may not be possible. In a case like this, you may want to quantify the alternatives by assigning numerical values to them on the basis of the extent to which they meet your established goals. The key idea here—and an essential concept that lies behind this entire chapter—is to evaluate your alternatives against established criteria rather than against one another.

The first thing to do when quantifying alternatives is to examine the goals that you identified when you explored the target dimension of the problem. Divide those goals into two groups: Group 1, which consists of the goals that absolutely *must be met* if the problem is to be solved, and Group 2, which consists of the goals that you *would like to meet* but that are not essential to the solution of the problem. Any alternative proposals that would not accomplish all of the goals in Group 1 should be eliminated immediately.

For example, if you were to use this method in buying a new car, you might proceed in this way: You have decided that the three things you absolutely *must have* in a car (your Group 1 goals or, in this case, criteria) are room for five passengers, a price tag of no more than $10,000, and a mileage rating of at least 30 miles per gallon on the highway. The things that you *would like to have* but that are not essential (your Group 2 criteria) include front-wheel drive, a sun roof, air conditioning, a six-cylinder engine, and an automatic transmission.

Naturally, you eliminate all available cars that do not meet the Group 1 criteria. Five cars, however, all of which you like, remain as possible candidates. You list the criteria in Group 2 from highest to lowest priority. Then you assign the highest priority the number 10 and assign the others lower numbers to reflect your estimate of their importance. In the new-car example, the priorities of the Group 2 goals might look something like this:

1. Front-wheel drive   = 10;
2. Air conditioning   = 8;
3. Standard transmission = 6;
4. Six-cylinder engine   = 6; and
5. Sun roof   = 2.

Next you measure the alternative proposals against each of these criteria. In the case of the five cars, this evaluation might appear as shown in Figure 15. After you have constructed a chart similar to the one in the figure, you simply total the points that each car earned. In this example Car A has 18, Car B 24, Car C 20, Car D 16, and Car E 16. Although this method will not make the decision for you, it does strongly suggest that in this instance Car B with 24 points most closely meets the established criteria.

This example, of course, is quite simple because the five candidates either have or do not have the various items desired. A more subtle example might involve the selection of three alternative actions or three candidates for an open position. Suppose that you are involved in selecting a new product for marketing and that you have identified five goals:

		Car A	Car B	Car C	Car D	Car E
Front-Wheel Drive	10	x	x		x	
Air Conditioning	8		x	x		x
Standard Transmission	6	x		x	x	x
Six-Cylinder Engine	6		x	x		
Sun Roof	2	x				x
Totals		18	24	20	16	16

Figure 15. Quantifying the Five Alternative Car Choices

1. Building greater overall consumer awareness of your company's products;
2. Establishing the new product in a specific consumer market;
3. Achieving gross sales for this new product of $700,000 within the next two months;
4. Producing a net profit of $120,000 for this new product within the next two months; and
5. Testing a new market strategy.

You decide that Goal 1 is essential and that if it is not accomplished the whole project will have failed. Then you review your company's new products and eliminate from consideration those that you feel would not significantly increase overall consumer awareness of the company's products. Three alternatives—Product A, Product B, and Product C—remain for consideration.

Next you weight the remaining four goals in terms of their importance. (Keep in mind that the highest-priority goal always is assigned the number 10.) The resulting list might appear as follows:

1. Establishing new product in specific market = 10;
2. Gross sales of $700,000 in two months = 8;
3. Net sales of $120,000 in two months = 7; and
4. Testing new marketing strategy = 3.

Suppose you felt that Product A would fully meet the second goal, would come fairly close to meeting the third, would have only a fifty-fifty chance of meeting the fourth, and had little chance of meeting the first. You would begin by assigning Product A the number 10 (the highest possible) on the second goal and lower numbers on the other three goals to reflect your estimate of how well Product A would meet those goals. That analysis might look like the one shown in Figure 16.

To obtain an overall numerical value for Product A, you would multiply the weighting of each goal by your estimate of the extent to which Product A would meet that goal (see Figure 17). After adding the four numbers resulting from this step, you would arrive at the total number of "points" earned by Product A, which is 171. Then you would follow the same procedure to determine the number of points earned by Products B and C. Finally, you would construct a chart of the completed analysis of all three products, which might look like the one shown in Figure 18. Although other factors may need to be taken into consideration, this particular analysis indicates that unless some strong case can be made against it, Product B should most likely be your choice.

		Product A
Specific Market	10	2
$700,000	8	10
$120,000	7	8
New Strategy	3	5

Figure 16. Analysis of Product A

		Product A	
Specific Market	10	2	(10 × 2 = 20)
$700,000	8	10	(8 × 10 = 80)
$120,000	7	8	(7 × 8 = 56)
New Strategy	3	5	(3 × 5 = 15)
Total			171

Figure 17. Obtaining a Numerical Value for Product A

There is one final variation of this method that can be used when you find that there is only one proposal left, but you are still not sure that this proposal is satisfactory. In this case you need to weigh that one alternative against an *ideal* solution. Suppose in the previous example you had only one product available instead of three. An ideal choice, of course, would rate a 10 on each goal; so you would incorporate these ideal ratings into the chart you construct and compare that ideal against the one product. Such a chart appears in Figure 19. Product A earned a total of 171 points against the ideal of 280; or, to put it another way, Product A is evaluated as 61 percent of the ideal. Then you would have to determine whether 61 percent of the ideal is acceptable. You may have to settle for this; but we would suggest that if the problem is at all significant, a solution that falls almost 40 percent short of being what you want may not be a very good idea. In such a case you may want to consider whether your goals are too ambitious or optimistic, or you may need to see if there is some way to improve Product A's performance against your criteria. If neither of these strategies works, you probably should go back to the proposal-generation stage and try to come up with something better.

		Product A	Product B	Product C
Specific Market	10	2 (20)	8 (80)	7 (70)
$700,000	8	10 (80)	6 (48)	9 (72)
$120,000	7	8 (56)	10 (70)	5 (35)
New Strategy	3	5 (15)	9 (27)	9 (27)
Totals		171	225	204

Figure 18. Quantifying Products A, B, and C

		Ideal	Product A
Specific Market	10	10 (100)	2 (20)
$700,000	8	10 (80)	10 (80)
$120,000	7	10 (70)	8 (56)
New Strategy	3	10 (30)	5 (15)
Totals		280	171

Figure 19. Comparison of Product A with an Ideal

Problem solving always involves degrees of uncertainty, but sometimes quantifying the alternatives will help you to move ahead with greater confidence. Be very cautious, however, about relying too heavily on this kind of analysis. The numbers can too often provide a false sense of security. They need to be understood for what they are: reflections of a series of estimates, guesses, and value choices. You should acknowledge directly the role that values play in your selection of a proposal; do not cover up the importance of values by pretending that you have based your decision solely on the apparent objectivity of numbers.

STEP 4: DECIDE

The purpose of problem solving is to take one or more actions that will change the current problem situation into something more closely resembling the desired state. At this point you must select a course of action. The selection will almost always be a judgment call. The evaluation of one proposal as more appropriate, attainable, attractive, or adaptable than another is not always easy. Information obtained from a pilot test may sometimes be ambiguous. Even the method we have just described for quantifying alternatives is less rational and scientific than might at first appear because the extent to which an alternative meets a particular goal is at best a guess. Nevertheless a choice must be made. If you have followed the process described in this book, you should be clear about what you are trying to accomplish; you should be confident that you understand the problem situation; and you will have explored a range of possible solutions. Your choice, therefore, will have the greatest possible chance of success when you finally act. The subject of planning, monitoring, and evaluating the implementation process is covered in the next chapter.

11

Making It Happen

From one point of view, when you reach the implementation stage you are almost at the end of the problem-solving process. Goals have been clarified; the situation, causes, and resources have been analyzed; proposals have been generated; and one or more solutions have been selected and are ready to be implemented. Little or nothing remains to be accomplished—except perhaps to congratulate yourself for having done such a careful job of problem analysis—before moving on to the next problem.

From another point of view, however, problem *management* has just begun. Few proposals can be implemented all at once or overnight, and the very process of implementation can itself generate both additional problems and new information. Implementing solutions to complex problems without planning, monitoring, and evaluating the implementation process amounts to little more than taking action, keeping your fingers crossed, and hoping for the best. Problem management is not complete until the problem actually has been managed and the process by which that management was accomplished has been evaluated.

STEP 1: PLAN FOR IMPLEMENTATION

At the end of Chapter 9, we suggested that one way to determine the relative worth of various proposals is to review them in terms of the *who, what, where, when, extent,* and *pattern* categories by asking the following questions:

- Who will do the work involved, and who will be affected by this proposal? What are the responses or reactions of those affected likely to be?

- What will this proposal accomplish, and what will be left to do after the proposal has been implemented?

- Where will this proposal be implemented, and where are difficulties in implementation likely to arise?

- When will this proposal be implemented, and when are difficulties in implementation likely to occur?

- Will this proposal completely or only partially reduce the extent of the problem or change the pattern of the problem?

At this point in the problem-solving process you have selected one or more solutions for implementation. Now you should return to these questions, this time to help guide your planning.

The first part of the planning process involves making sure that you understand exactly what it is you want to have happen. In some situations this will be quite simple. In the case study involving Alder Lumber Company, for example, Bert planned to talk with the shop steward and have him, in turn, talk with Bob about Bob's responsibilities as a union member. In that case the planning process may have taken as much as a minute or so. In other, more complex, cases, however, you may wish to lay out in writing and in some detail a step-by-step action plan, including people, dates, times, and places. The steps outlined in "A Planning Process" in the Appendix of this book may prove helpful in doing that.

The second part of the planning process consists of analyzing carefully what might go wrong. Of course, you cannot plan for every contingency; and it probably would be a waste of time to try to do so. Instead, identify the steps or points in your plan that will be most difficult to accomplish, those about which you are least confident, or those that you feel will leave you the most vulnerable. Then, using the categories *who, what, where, when, extent,* and *pattern*, identify potential problems as clearly as possible.

Once you have identified these problems, use what you have learned in this book and follow these three steps (Kepner & Tregoe, 1981) to address each problem:

1. Analyze the potential problem in terms of causes, resources, and solutions.

2. Identify actions that you intend to take in advance to prevent the problem.

3. Identify actions that you intend to take if and when the problem develops.

This kind of contingency planning can have rich payoffs in terms of both avoiding trouble and attaining peace of mind.

Unfortunately, as you have seen, implementation is the point to which people typically leap soon after being confronted with a problem. As often as not, difficulties develop during implementation because of inadequate problem analysis rather than inadequate skills. Integrated problem management has been designed to prepare the problem solver not for just any action, but for those actions that are most likely to solve the problem. Consequently, you may now act with confidence.

STEP 2: MONITOR THE IMPLEMENTATION PROCESS

Proposals are intended to change the current situation into the target. But just as few proposals can be implemented all at once, few problem situations transform themselves into the desired state in an instant. The path from situation to target is often a long and complicated journey. The first and most important reason for monitoring the implementation of a proposal, therefore, is to help ensure that you are moving with reasonable speed toward a solution.

Your actions, however, are likely to generate new situational information, to further clarify your values, and to sharpen your ideas about solving the problem. In other words, any action changes the current situation in ways that may require the collection of additional information, a re-examination of goals, or a reconsideration of proposals. The second reason for monitoring proposal implementation, consequently, is to stay in touch with any changes that your actions may have caused in the domains of information, values, and ideas. The problem as presented may be quite different from the problem as understood halfway through the process of implementation.

STEP 3: EVALUATE YOUR EXPERIENCES

Finally, if you are to learn from your problem-solving experience, you must from time to time step back from that experience and evaluate the problem-solving process itself. The first evaluation task is to reflect as impartially as possible on what actually has happened. Judgments about your successes and failures should be made on the basis of careful observation and reflection rather than feelings or intuition. Also, you should be less concerned with how other people feel about what has happened than with your own rational assessment.

The second evaluation task is to examine your current and past problem-solving experiences to see if there are general patterns, themes, or tendencies. Every person who uses integrated problem management to some extent develops his or her own unique version of that process, and learning what your approach is will be useful to you in future problem-solving efforts. Finally, you need to answer these two questions: "What have I learned about problem solving from working on this particular problem?" and "How do I plan to solve my next problem?" Following this procedure of evaluating— as well as that of monitoring—will enable you to become truly proficient in the process of integrated problem management.

REFERENCE

Kepner, C.H., & Tregoe, B.B. (1981). *The new rational manager.* Princeton, NJ: Kepner-Tregoe, Inc.

12

Situation, Target, and Proposal: Interactive Dimensions

At the beginning of this book we suggested that although situation, target, and proposal share a very close connection, we would proceed as if problem solving were a step-by-step process moving from an identification of the target (values) through an analysis of the situation (information) to the generation and selection of one or more proposals (ideas). It is now time to return to that close connection and explore the way in which these three dimensions interact in most "real-life" problem-management efforts.

It is certainly true that problem management may at times move in a step-by-step manner from target to situation to proposal. Because these three dimensions are not independent of one another, however, problem management is best thought of not as a movement from one dimension to another but rather as an interaction among all three. Their common interrelationships are described in Table 1.

**Table 1. Interrelationships
of Situation, Target, and Proposal**

Interrelationship	How the Dimensions Interrelate
Situation and Target	Dissatisfaction with the situation implies a particular target.
	Any suggested target implies something about what is wrong with the current situation.
Target and Proposal	A target defines the results desired from any proposal.
	Any proposal embodies assumptions about the nature of the desired target.
Situation and Proposal	The situation places limits on the effectiveness and feasibility of acceptable proposals.
	A proposal embodies assumptions about the causes of the unsatisfactory situation and implies resources and requirements for change.

Because of these interrelationships, it is often effective to work on all three dimensions at once rather than one at a time. In managing a problem you should feel free to generate and develop data about each dimension as appropriate. Your exploration of the problem can be spontaneous, but what you learn or discover should be recorded in three separate columns if you are working alone or on three separate sheets of newsprint if you are working with a group. Entries can be made in the appropriate categories as data are collected and accepted as valid or legitimate.

Because each dimension is related to the others, it is possible to translate statements about one dimension into statements that are relevant to the other dimensions. When information is generated about the situation, for example, values can be elicited by asking questions such as these:

- If I could change the present situation, what would I want to accomplish?

- What is missing in the present situation that I want?

- What would be my goal in improving the situation?

Proposals can be generated from that same situational statement by asking questions such as these:

- What might be done to improve the situation?

- What kind of action does the situation seem to require?

- What plan would use the resources that I have identified?

When a target has been identified, situational information can be elicited by asking these questions:

- In what ways does the present situation fall short of the goal?

- Why does the present situation fall short of the goal?

- What forces for improvement exist for reaching the goal?

- What obstacles stand in the way of reaching the goal?

Proposals can be elicited from the same target statement by asking:

- What might be a possible way to accomplish the goal?

- What steps might lead toward the goal?

Similarly, when a proposal presents itself, situational information can be elicited by asking:

- In what ways might the proposal improve the present situation?

- What part of the problem does the proposal deal with?

- What resources exist for implementing the proposal?

Finally, values can be elicited from a proposal by asking:

- What would the proposal accomplish?

- What objective does the proposal address?

Problem solving often seems to wander aimlessly from topic to topic without ever actually coming to grips with the problem at hand. By categorizing statements according to situation, target, or proposal and by using statements in one dimension to produce greater clarity in the other dimensions, you can use integrated problem management as a flexible and responsive strategy rather than a series of rigid steps moving from one dimension to the next.

13

Implementing the Situation-Target-Proposal Model

The Situation-Target-Proposal Model can be used successfully at any of three levels: individual, group, and organizational. However, using the model requires a change in the way in which people attempt to solve problems. In this final chapter we make some suggestions about how to go about using the model and effecting the necessary change at each level.

USING THE MODEL AT THE INDIVIDUAL LEVEL

Someone once said that if you want to change the world, you should begin by cleaning out your own closet. We believe that this saying also applies to trying new approaches such as integrated problem management. Just as cleaning your closet often means that you must throw away a lot of useless items (including some that you may be fond of), so too does mental closet cleaning in preparation for trying something new require that you discard some of your old, familiar patterns of thinking and behaving.

The following four steps may help you when you attempt to use the model on your own:

1. *Develop commitment.* Making integrated problem management as effective for yourself as it can be requires personal commitment to the process. One way to help establish this commitment is to write on an index card the following statement: *At least once a week for the next eight weeks I will use the Situation-Target-Proposal Model to address a personal or professional problem.* Below this statement list the weeks separately. Then, once a week and at the same time each week, refer to the index card and record the ways in which you have used the model, the successes you have had, and any difficulties you might have encountered. By the end of the eight-week period you should be well on the way to making integrated problem management a normal part of your approach to problems.

2. *Study.* Become very familiar with the contents of this book. Start with reviewing your scores on The Problem-Solving Style Inventory (p. 25). Do you tend to be a realist, an idealist, an activist, or a pragmatist? What are the pitfalls involved in your

particular approach to problem solving? Next skim through Chapters 6 through 11, noting which parts of the problem-solving process outlined in those chapters seemed the most comfortable to you and which seemed the most difficult or the most different from your usual approach to problem solving. Finally, review the questions listed in Chapter 12, noting which sound familiar because you are accustomed to asking them and which you need to ask more often. This review process should help you to focus on those parts of this book to which you need to pay particular attention.

3. **Accept occasional failures.** In attempting to change some of the fundamental ways in which you think and behave, do not expect yourself to make these changes quickly or easily. Even though we have written this book and have had years of experience with this material, we still find ourselves from time to time taking action without adequate planning, rushing to implement the first proposal that presents itself, or acting without a clear sense of the target. No one is perfect; do not be too hard on yourself if you find that you are not always able to use the process outlined in this book.

4. **Look for training possibilities.** Your attempts to learn new ways of thinking and behaving can be supported and reinforced by working with others. Consider participating in workshops and seminars on problem solving that look interesting. You should be able to incorporate what you learn in those workshops into your use of the Situation-Target-Proposal Model. We also recommend workshops on value clarification. Most problem-solving models do not devote enough attention to what we have called the domain of values, and workshops on values can be particularly helpful in learning how to work more effectively in that domain.

As consultants to a variety of groups and organizations, we often find ourselves working with others on their problems. Occasionally, if the time is available, we teach them the basics of the Situation-Target-Proposal Model. But more often than not we simply ask the right questions in terms of situation, target, and proposal. By using the model, but without ever explaining it or mentioning the terms, we have helped hundreds of groups and organizations to solve their own problems. We think that you can make progress in your own attempts to use the model, even when you must work with another person or a group of people who are totally unfamiliar with the process.

Reread the conversation between Bill and Larry in Chapter 3. Do you see how Bill is using the model and how little of the process outlined in this book needs to be explained to Larry to help him work through his problem with Frank? Think, too, of the way in which Bert at Alder Lumber Company handled his problems with Bob, Steve, and Don. None of the other three men knew anything about the Situation-Target-Proposal Model, but Bert nevertheless used it effectively in solving both his machine and people problems.

The key to making this work for you is to learn the process we have outlined and then use the "Twenty Useful Questions in Integrated Problem Management" on page ix. You probably looked at those questions when you first picked up this book, and they probably did not make much sense to you at that time. But now they do, and the page on which they are printed may well be the most important and valuable page in this entire book. Learn those questions and use them; doing so will enable you to become a more effective and successful problem solver.

USING THE MODEL AT THE GROUP LEVEL

To begin this section we want to relate one of our consulting adventures. This story is embarrassing from a consultant's point of view, but it taught us a lot about group functioning and group problem solving. A small but prosperous company was undergoing a transition into an important, professionally managed corporation. As a result of this transition, the president of the company had come to realize that he needed to develop his top-management group into an effective team. In the past most of this group's work had been done in informal, "hallway" meetings of two or three individuals; and, of course, conducting business in this way meant that most of the group members did not know what was going on most of the time. Attempts at formal, regularly scheduled meetings ended either in shouting matches or in boredom and inaction. The president knew that something needed to be done and asked for our help.

We used team building to address this situation. The president identified ten managers as belonging to his top-management group, and we interviewed all ten people to find out their perceptions of the problem. We then reported the resulting information to the total group. Over a period of several months, we taught these managers how to hold effective meetings. We instructed them on the use of some of the most powerful management tools available in our field today. We worked through all of the old conflicts and hidden agendas that had kept the members at odds for so many years.

Then in their first, formal, regularly scheduled top-management meeting, we turned them loose on the major problems facing the company. They struggled and floundered, making almost no progress. They shared agendas; they listened to each other; they liked each other; and they were trying. But the meeting was unsuccessful; and it was painful for us to watch, both because we cared for them as people and, of course, because their struggle reflected on our work with them.

What was wrong? Both of us knew the answer theoretically; but that was the day we learned the answer in a very real, practical way. In any group three kinds of issues exist at the same time. The first kind is *task* issues that relate directly to accomplishing the goals defined by the group as its reason for being. Examples of task issues include how to market a new product, how to trim 5 percent from the operating budget, and whether to approve a particular research project. The second kind is *process* issues, which are related to both the relationships that exist among the members of the group and the feelings brought into the group or developed during its meetings. Examples of process issues include whether the group members like working with one another, how the remaining members feel when one of the members behaves aggressively, and how individual members feel about the way in which their ideas are received by the other members. The third kind is *method* issues, which specifically focus on the means by which the group accomplishes a task. Method issues include such things as how the group members share information, how they handle a meeting agenda, and how they solve problems and make decisions in the group.

What we had done wrong with this group quickly became obvious. We had helped the members clarify their *task* concerns, and we had spent a great deal of our time helping them work through and perform more effectively at the *process* level. But we had not provided the group with an effective *method* for working on its tasks.

The lesson here is an important one. In *some* groups the members do not work well together because they either do not know what their task is or, if they do know, they lack the needed expertise. In *many* groups the members do not work well together because they do not communicate effectively with one another. But in *most* groups the members have difficulty because they do not have a shared and commonly understood method for solving problems and making decisions.

If you are in a position to influence a group of which you are either the leader or a member, you can help the members to begin using the Situation-Target-Proposal Model by showing them this book. If they like it, you might provide each of them with a copy and have them read the book and bring their copies to the group's meetings. Then take some time during your meetings to discuss each of the chapters. Have one member at each meeting be responsible for asking the appropriate question from the "Twenty Useful Questions in Integrated Problem Management" when needed. At the end of each meeting, take ten minutes to review the way in which the group used (or forgot to use) the model.

Change is always difficult. Even though one person who knows these concepts can be of great help to a group, the effect of the concepts is multiplied as each member tries them and supports and reinforces the attempts of others to use integrated problem management. Consequently, we encourage you to recommend the process to the other members of your group. To help the top-management group that was floundering despite our team-building efforts, we arranged to teach the members how to use integrated problem management. Once the group had a *method* to complement its resolved *task* and *process* issues, it became much more effective and has since provided significant leadership and direction for an increasingly successful corporation.

USING THE MODEL AT THE ORGANIZATIONAL LEVEL

Much has been written in recent years about organizational culture. Each organization, much like a small country, has its own unique patterns of dressing, talking, writing, and working. Even in the same business or industry, different organizations may have significantly different cultures.

Previously we said that when all members of a group begin using the Situation-Target-Proposal Model, the group becomes more effective. The same is true of an organization. But changing an organization's problem-solving patterns means changing its culture, and that is not an easy task. However, the following guidelines can be of help:

1. **Start at the top.** The idea of starting change at the grass-roots level seems to be attractive to many, but by and large this approach does not work as a change strategy in organizations. People at the top of the hierarchy not only must be seen by others in the organization as supportive of the change effort, but also must be actively involved in that process. The first group in any organization to learn integrated problem management should be the top-management team. The process of implementing the Situation-Target-Proposal Model should proceed no further until that group is comfortable with integrated problem management and is actually using it on a regular basis.

2. **Focus on natural work groups.** As we mentioned before, a group can effect change more easily if its members support and reinforce one another; and the suggestions we made about implementing integrated problem management at the group level

are also relevant for an organization. Once the top-management group is using the Situation-Target-Proposal Model, the next ones to learn the process should be the natural work groups reporting to the top managers, who can support and reinforce their managers in the use of the process. Training can proceed downward through the organization in this fashion, always within natural work groups.

3. ***Do not ignore task and process.*** If the natural work groups do not have a clear idea of what their tasks are, do not have the expertise to complete these tasks, or do not work well at an interpersonal level, they are not likely to make very effective use of integrated problem management. In situations in which there are serious concerns at the task and process levels, team building should be conducted prior to training in how to use the Situation-Target-Proposal Model.

4. ***Be patient.*** Organizational change takes time. In small companies the widespread and successful use of the Situation-Target-Proposal Model may take several months to achieve, and in large companies it may take a year or more. Creating an organizational culture takes years, so changing it within a few weeks is a very unlikely possibility.

IN CONCLUSION

You have come a long way from the first couple of chapters of this book. Remember some of the examples of poor problem solving presented in Chapter 1: the case of the government forms and the workshop that did not address the cause of the problem, the case of the private university in New York that had to scrap its ten-year plan less than two years after it was written, and the case of the vacationing couple who biked halfway across the country to see a ship and then discovered that the ship was somewhere else. Also, you will recall that Larry and Bill's first attempt to solve the problem with Frank was unsuccessful.

But now you are unlikely to make mistakes such as these because you know how to use integrated problem management. If you are working alone on a problem, you will think through situation, target, and proposal before taking action. If you are working with others, you will become a consultant to them by asking the right questions to solve the problem.

Perhaps you are in a position to help an entire group learn how to use integrated problem management; you may even be influential enough to set in motion the steps needed to make the Situation-Target-Proposal Model a part of your organization's culture. Wherever you find yourself, we are confident that the use of integrated problem management can contribute significantly to your ability to manage and control your personal and professional lives. We have defined problem solving as the process of changing the world from the way things are now to the way people would like them to be, and we think you will agree that bringing about that kind of change is a useful way to spend your time. The rest is up to you.

Appendix

Setting Priorities

As discussed in Chapter 6, most problems do not have a single goal. Instead, people are likely to encounter a number of goals associated with a single target. Consequently, a key step in working in the target dimension is the establishment of clear priorities among those several goals. Because priorities reflect values and because people's values differ, setting priorities in groups is sometimes difficult. The following activity[9] has been found helpful to groups that are having difficulty clarifying their goals or deciding which goal has the highest priority.

Once the problem has been identified, the group members are asked to assemble into pairs and for ten minutes (five minutes per person) interview each other about what each sees as the major goals that he or she would like to accomplish in solving the problem. These interviews allow the members an opportunity to clarify and focus their thinking, and the time limit forces them to focus on what they see as the most important goals. After the interviews have been completed, the group leader or facilitator asks each pair to report: One of the members announces the goals identified by his or her partner, who corrects or modifies this information if desired and then reports on the goals identified by the other person, who is also given a chance to correct as necessary. This process is continued until all pairs have identified their goals. During the reporting process all goals are listed on newsprint; each goal is assigned a letter, and similar goals are combined if possible.

Each group member is next asked to identify privately what he or she feels to be the top three goals on the newsprint list. The group leader or facilitator asks the members to take turns announcing their votes while he or she tallies the results on the newsprint. The top-ranked goals—usually no more than six to eight—are then listed by letter on a separate sheet of newsprint. Then the members are asked again to privately rank order the remaining goals in terms of what they see as their priority, beginning with 1 as the highest priority. Using a grid like the one presented in Figure 20, the leader or facilitator polls the members by asking how many ranked each of the listed goals as first priority, second priority, and so forth, and by placing the total number in each box as appropriate. A final listing of goals in order of priority then can be developed from that ranking.

---

[9]This activity is based on "Agenda Setting: A Team-Building Starter" in *A Handbook of Structured Experiences for Human Relations Training*, Vol. V (pp. 108-110) by J.W. Pfeiffer and J.E. Jones (Eds.), 1975, San Diego, CA: University Associates. Copyright 1975 by International Authors, B.V. Adapted by permission.

Priority

	1st	2nd	3rd	4th	5th	6th	7th	8th
C								
D								
H								
P								
W								
AA								
FF								
II								

Figure 20. Grid for Polling About the Ranking of Goals

REFERENCE

Pfeiffer, J.W., & Jones, J.E. (Eds.) (1975). *A handbook of structured experiences for human relations training* (Vol. V.). San Diego, CA: University Associates.

Cross-Impact Analysis

Sometimes your goals may be quite clear but their priorities quite unclear. In such cases a cross-impact analysis may be of assistance in determining priorities. This approach has an additional advantage in that it can be used by an individual as well as a group.

Furthermore, a cross-impact analysis can be used to help determine the relative values of several goals in terms of their potential "enabling" capacity, that is, their capacity to increase the probability that one or more other desired goals will be attained. This concept of enabling capacity may help to break a deadlock in deliberations concerning two or more goals. It allows those working on the problem to acknowledge the value of each of several goals, while selecting for immediate attention the one goal that is not only valuable in and of itself but also valuable as a vehicle for enabling other goals to be achieved.

To perform a cross-impact analysis, first construct a matrix with each of several goals listed both vertically and horizontally. Assume, for example, that the four goals being considered are the following:

1. The purchase and installation of a new computer;
2. The implementation of a new budgeting system for the sales department;
3. The hiring of a third account manager; and
4. The reformulation of the performance-appraisal system for the accounting department.

In this case the matrix would look like the one illustrated in Figure 21.

The cross-impact analysis is performed by determining whether each goal listed vertically would tend to increase, decrease, or have no impact on the probable achievement of each of the other goals listed horizontally. In the example a determination would be made as to whether the new computer (Goal 1) would increase, decrease, or have no impact on the implementation of the new budgeting system for the sales department (Goal 2), on the hiring of a new account manager (Goal 3), and on the reformulation of the performance-appraisal system (Goal 4). If the computer would increase the probability of achieving any of these other three goals, a plus sign (+) would be written in the appropriate cell on the first horizontal line, which is labeled *1. New Computer.* If it would decrease the probability, a minus (–) sign would be written in the appropriate cell. A zero (0) designates little or no impact or influence. Figure 22 illustrates the outcome of this process. The new computer would have no impact on refor-

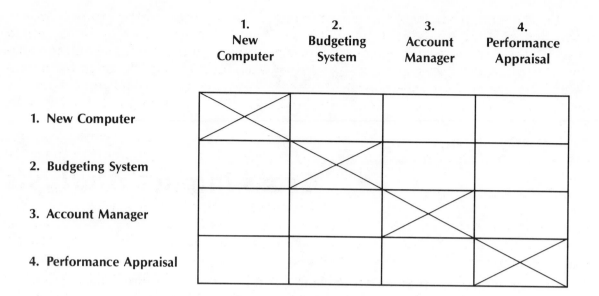

Figure 21. Example of Cross-Impact Analysis
(Construction of Matrix)

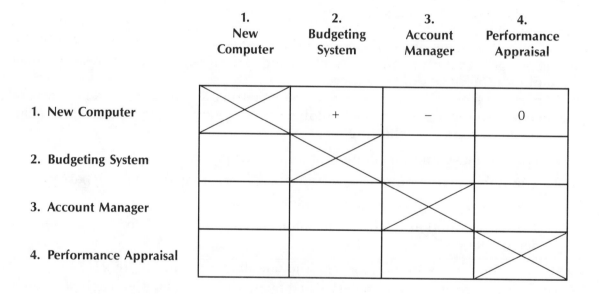

Figure 22. Example of Cross-Impact Analysis
(Goal 1 Analysis)

mulating the performance-appraisal system, would increase the probability of implementing the new budget system for sales, and would decrease the probability of hiring a third account manager.

Then a similar analysis for the second goal is completed. In the example we are using, a successful implementation of the new budgeting system would be examined to see if it would increase, decrease, or have no impact on the purchase and installation of the new computer, the hiring of a third account manager, or the implementation of the new performance-appraisal system. Subsequently, Goals 3 and 4 would be analyzed in the same way. A completed analysis would resemble that illustrated in Figure 23.

The matrix produced by this analysis should be examined to determine which of the goals demonstrate maximum enabling capacity, that is, which increase the probable achievement of the greatest number of other goals. In our example, one goal (the implementation of a new budgeting system) has an enabling (+) impact on two other goals. The matrix does not indicate that the new budgeting system is necessarily more important than the other two; but it does indicate that if difficulty is being experienced in establishing priorities, the budgeting system might be selected because of its enabling features as well as for its inherent value.

A cross-impact analysis also provides a sense of the relationship among various projects. In our example it becomes immediately apparent that the proposed performance-appraisal system is unrelated to any of the other three goals, whereas the other three goals are at least somewhat interrelated, with the new computer and the budgeting system being closely linked in a positive, enabling manner. When a large number of zeroes appear on a cross-impact matrix, many separate goals and projects exist. Efforts should be made to bring these projects closer together. Some joint planning or combining of goals might be appropriate. If a large number of positive relationships exist, then the issue may be one of determining where to start. Everything is related to everything else, and almost any starting place will do. Some negotiation and compromise may be appropriate, with emphasis being placed on the mutual enabling of the various projects.

	1. New Computer	2. Budgeting System	3. Account Manager	4. Performance Appraisal
1. New Computer		+	−	0
2. Budgeting System	+		+	0
3. Account Manager	−	0		0
4. Performance Appraisal	0	0	0	

Figure 23. Example of Cross-Impact Analysis
(Completed)

A large number of negative relationships indicate that a "win/lose" situation exists. Whatever one goal wins, the others lose. This situation can be very destructive; if various parties are involved in the situation, they should be called together to identify areas of shared interest and concern. New resources (money, time, and personnel) might also be identified so that the various goals are not always competing against one another for scarce resources. Unfortunately, this latter solution to a negative cross-impact field is not always realistic. Often a more difficult route must be taken: Several goals must be eliminated so that sufficient resources will be available to achieve the remaining goal or goals.

With the completion and review of the cross-impact matrix, choices can be made among several different goals based not only on an assessment of the relative worth of each goal considered in isolation, but also on the basis of its worth as related to the potential impact on the achievement of other goals. Target conflicts often can be resolved through the use of this kind of analysis.

Five Ways to Obtain Information

Although there are many different ways to obtain information in most situations, the five described below are the most commonly and easily used.

1. **Interviewing.** This is probably the most widely used and generally most appropriate method of information collection. Interviews can be conducted individually or in small groups. Sometimes they are open ended in that the responses to initial questions (usually determined ahead of time) dictate the nature and scope of later questions. At other times the questions might all be specified prior to the interview. Relatively brief, structured interviews are useful for obtaining factual information, while more open-ended approaches are suitable for collecting more subjective information.

2. **Administering a questionnaire.** Questionnaires can be used almost as frequently as interviews. Sometimes a questionnaire can be developed that specifically focuses on the problem situation. At other times a standard questionnaire can be used to reduce the time needed to develop your own.

3. **Observing.** Although observation is time consuming, it can provide real insight into the nature of the problem. If the problem can be observed as it actually is taking place, it will be more likely to be understood.

4. **Reviewing documents.** Written information about the problem may be collected and reviewed. Some documents should be read carefully, especially those concerning goals, policies, production, and outcomes related to the problem situation. Additional documents can be reviewed more quickly for broad themes or unique perceptions and insights.

5. **Reviewing general information.** One of the most important sources of information resides in you, in the memory and experience of the person working on the problem. Information about the history of the problem, trends, experiences with similar problems, general practices, and so forth all can be useful in understanding the current situation. When working on a problem, you should always consider such pieces of information because creative solutions often build on them.

Force-Field Analysis

We discuss force-field analysis in this appendix for two reasons: First, it is a basic and very powerful problem-solving tool, and it would be almost unheard of to write a book on problem solving without describing how to conduct such an analysis; second, we want you to see how this kind of analysis lies behind causal/resource analysis. When we ask you to examine similarities and differences between the problem situation and the comparative situation and then to identify causes and resources, we are actually drawing on the technique of force-field analysis. Knowing how to conduct such an analysis will help you to understand more fully what your objective is at that point in the problem-solving process.

Force-field analysis[10] was developed by Kurt Lewin, one of the founding fathers of the entire field of applied behavioral science. Lewin was trained as a physicist and applied that background to the description of social systems. The basic idea behind force-field analysis is that any social situation, including a problem situation, can be described as being made up of a series of vectors or forces, some pushing for change, some resisting change. If the total forces for change equal the total forces opposing change, there will be no movement or change in the status quo. A force-field analysis is simply an analysis of those vectors or forces.

When we present force-field analysis in our workshops, we ask each participant to draw a diagram like the one presented in Figure 24. Down the left side of the diagram each participant lists the forces that are driving the present problem toward solution or resolution. These may be forces external to the individual problem solver, such as company policy, the pressure of competition, technological developments, and so forth; they may also be internal or psychological forces like motivation, commitment, or skills. The estimated strength of each force is indicated by the length of the arrow or vector assigned to it.

Once the driving forces have been listed, each participant lists blocking or restraining forces, the forces that are preventing movement toward solution, down the right side of the diagram. Again, these may be either external or internal forces; and, again, the length of each arrow represents the estimated strength of that force.

---

[10]For the original presentation of force-field analysis, see *Field Theory in Social Science* by K. Lewin, 1951, New York: Harper & Row.

Target:

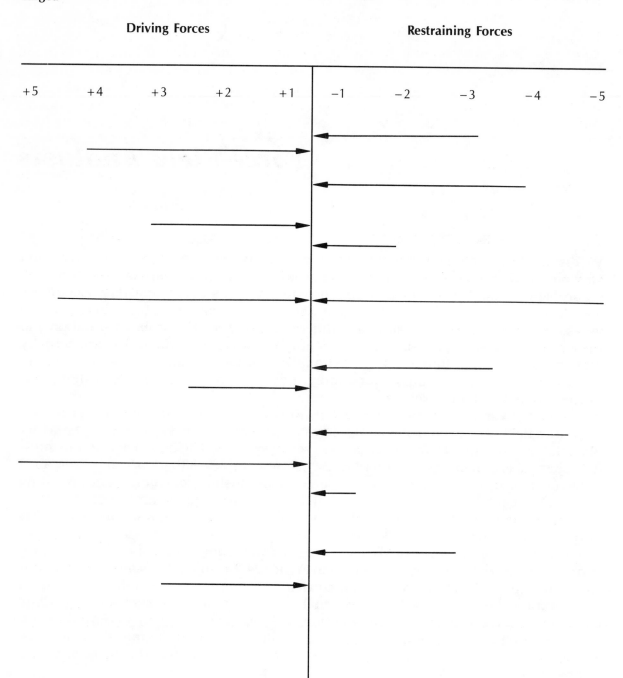

Driving Forces

Restraining Forces

| +5 | +4 | +3 | +2 | +1 | −1 | −2 | −3 | −4 | −5 |

Figure 24. A Diagram of Force-Field Analysis

It is at this point that force-field analysis connects with causal/resource analysis. We have come to realize that the positive forces identified by a force-field analysis are often identical to the similarities generated by comparing the problem situation with the comparative situation; also, we have discovered that the resources for solution of a problem lie in those positive forces or similarities. In a similar manner, we have come to realize that the restraining forces are frequently identical to the differences between the problem and comparative situations and that in the list of differences must lie the cause or causes of a problem. Lewin's force-field analysis has helped to confirm in our own minds what we were trying to accomplish in conducting causal/resource analysis.

We tend to prefer causal/resource analysis to force-field analysis because the former is preceded by a careful assessment of both the problem situation and the comparative situation, while the latter simply assumes that an understanding of the differences between these two situations exists. Nevertheless, we believe that you might find force-field analysis useful on those occasions when you are having trouble with causal/resource analysis or when you want to take a quick pass at your problem to see what additional insights you might be able to generate.

Once both driving and restraining forces have been listed, a rough estimate should be made of their relative strengths. One of three conditions will result: The driving forces will outweigh the restraining forces; the restraining forces will outweigh the driving forces; or the two sets of forces will be roughly equal. These three conditions suggest three different strategies in moving toward problem solution.

If the driving forces clearly outweigh the restraining forces, simply proceed. The prediction is that you are going to be successful in solving your problem. If the restraining forces heavily outweigh the driving forces, however, you should either be very patient or reconsider your target. With all of those restraining forces against you, it may be unrealistic to think that you can solve the problem, at least as you have defined it so far. You may want to "go back to the drawing board" to identify a smaller but more realistic piece of the problem to attack, at least for the time being.

Finally, if the restraining and driving forces are about equal, we suggest that you resist the natural tendency to push harder on the driving forces. This approach may work from time to time, but in our experience what happens more often is that the harder we push, the harder the restraining forces seem to push back all by themselves. Consequently, we put a lot more energy into our field of forces but find that we are making no progress.

Instead, we suggest that you look at the restraining forces and identify those that can be weakened or eliminated. If you are able to affect the restraining forces in this way, you will not need to add new driving forces because you will have created an imbalance in which the driving forces outweigh the restraining forces. In this case you will begin to move toward solution.

We think you will find a force-field analysis useful when working on those problems in which you are clear about your target and you have a firm grasp of the facts of the problem situation. If you are uncertain about the target or the problem situation, we suggest you go through the process described in Chapters 6 and 7. If the cause of the problem is unknown, the process of causal/resource analysis will work better for you. But do not be afraid to try force-field analysis occasionally; you may well come up with some new ideas for the solution of a problem.

REFERENCE

Lewin, K. (1951). *Field theory in social science*. New York: Harper & Row.

Fifty Questions

In addition to the questions suggested in Chapter 7 and elsewhere in this book, you might want to consider the following fifty questions from Arthur B. Van Gundy's (1983) *108 Ways to Get a Bright Idea:*[11]

1. Who is affected by the problem?
2. Who else has the problem?
3. Who decided that the situation is a problem?
4. Who would be happy if the problem was solved?
5. Who would be sad if the problem was solved?
6. Who could prevent the problem from being solved?
7. Who needs to solve the problem more than you?

8. What do you think will change about the problem?
9. What are the problem's major weaknesses?
10. What do you like about the problem?
11. What do you dislike about the problem?
12. What can be changed about the problem?
13. What can't be changed about the problem?
14. What do you know about the problem?
15. What don't you know about the problem?

---

[11]From the book *108 Ways to Get a Bright Idea* (pp. 86-87) by Arthur B. Van Gundy, © 1983. Used by permission of the publisher, Prentice-Hall, Inc./Simon & Schuster, Englewood Cliffs, New Jersey.

16. What will it be like if the problem is solved?
17. What will it be like if the problem isn't solved?
18. What have you done in the past with similar problems?
19. What is the principle underlying the problem?
20. What value systems underlie the problem?
21. What problem elements are related to one another?
22. What assumptions are you making about the problem?
23. What seems to be most important about the problem?
24. What seems to be least important about the problem?
25. What subproblems are there?
26. What are your major objectives in solving the problem?
27. What else do you need to know about the problem?

28. Where is the problem most noticeable?
29. Where is the problem least noticeable?
30. Where else does the problem exist?
31. Where is the best place to begin looking for solutions?
32. Where does the problem fit in the larger scheme of things?

33. When does the problem occur?
34. When doesn't the problem occur?
35. When did the problem first become a problem?
36. When will the problem stop being a problem?
37. When do other people see your problem as a problem?
38. When don't other people see your problem as a problem?
39. When does the problem need to be solved?
40. When is the problem likely to occur again?
41. When will the problem get worse?
42. When will the problem get better?

43. Why is this situation a problem?
44. Why do you want to solve the problem?
45. Why don't you want to solve the problem?
46. Why doesn't the problem go away?
47. Why would someone else want to solve the problem?
48. Why wouldn't someone else want to solve the problem?

49. Why is the problem easy to solve?

50. Why is the problem hard to solve?

Problem solving may be nothing more than the art of asking the right questions at the right time. We feel that the categories *who, what, where, when, extent,* and *pattern* cover the problem situation well, but we also like a number of these fifty questions as ways of stimulating thinking and enhancing understanding about a problem. Obviously, do not try to use all fifty with any single problem, but do consider some of the ones that seem relevant.

REFERENCE

Van Gundy, A.B. (1983). *108 ways to get a bright idea*. Englewood Cliffs, NJ: Prentice-Hall.

A Planning Process

1. Summarize the plan of action you intend to take in a few sentences or, at most, a single paragraph.

2. What do you intend to accomplish through this plan? When do you intend to begin and end the implementation of the plan?

3. What are the specific steps you will need to take to accomplish your plan?

4. What assumptions or events about which you do not have certain information may affect your plan as it unfolds? In what ways might you obtain that information before beginning your plan?

5. What resources do you have or will you need to carry out your plan? (Resources include time, energy, skills, commitment, experience—anyone or anything available to help you with your plan.)

Resources I have:

Resources I will need:

6. What limitations or barriers do you face in carrying out your plan? Which of these barriers can be weakened or eliminated?

7. What tasks or action steps need to be taken according to what schedule to put your plan in action?

8. Implementation: Proceed!

9. Evaluation: How successful were you? Did you encounter any unexpected difficulties? Do you now have any new information that might enable you to recycle through this planning process? What is your next plan?